LIVING DREAMS

LIVING LIFE

A PRACTICAL GUIDE
to understanding your dreams
and how they can
change your waking life

UPDATED SECOND EDITION

EVELYN M. DUESBURY

All the dreams and interpretations presented in this book are reprinted with permission by the dreamers.

Original Copyright © 2007 by Steven L. Duesbury. All Rights Reserved. Revised Edition published 2019

_____

No part of this book may be reproduced or transmitted in any form or by any means, graphic, electronic, or mechanical, including photocopying, recording, taping, or by any information storage or retrieval system, without the permission in writing from the publisher.

Cover art by Evelyn M. Duesbury
(Living Stream, Living Tree, Living Dreams, Living Life)

DEDICATION

This book is dedicated to all the dreamers who contributed dreams and interpretations during research projects; their work with their dreams gave wings to the PMID model

Endorsements from Professionals

"*Living Dreams, Living Life* is a breath of fresh air to readers interested in working with their dreams. Its author presents a practical method for sifting through the layers of metaphors and symbols to arrive at a dream's surprisingly direct counsel on solving problems, improving relationships, and enhancing creative spiritual growth."
--Stanley Krippner, Ph.D.,
Co-Author, *Extraordinary Dreams and How to Work with Them*

"The PMID method for unfolding the enfolded meaning of the dream is a beautiful fusion of ancient dreamwork styles with the new, personalized methods that appreciate the unique inner-landscape of the person and their familial dynamics. The method is an effective tool in understanding emotional health issues connected with familial dynamics."
--Edward Bruce Bynum, Ph.D.
Author, *Families and the Interpretation of Dreams.*

"You are right that it [PMID model] is very consistent with my article, 'Making Connections in a Safe Place: Is Dreaming Psychotherapy?' In fact, you seem to have done a brilliant job of using your dreams as psychotherapy and being your own therapist through the use of your dreams."
-- Excerpt of letter from Ernest Hartmann, M. D.
Author of *Dreams and Nightmares.*

"I believe the PMID approach is a psychologically sound one . . . and is one that can be taught to others fairly easily. Through use of this approach, a dreamer could be guided to understand better the complex patterns of emotions and attitudes that become interwoven between significant individuals being dealt with by the dreamer in the realm of their interpersonal relationships."

--Robert L. Van de Castle, Ph. D.
Author, *Our Dreaming Mind*

Contents

SECTION	PAGE

Section A: Introduction to *Living Dreams, Living Life*   1

    Chapter 1: The Personalized Method for Interpreting Dreams (PMID) -- Preliminary Work   11

Section B: Living Dreams, Finding Answers with the PMID Model   17

    Alice's Dream: Dad and the Inventory   18

    Chapter 2: What's Happening in Your Life? PMID Step 1   20

    Chapter 3: What's on Your Mind? PMID Step 2   26

    Chapter 4: What's the Connection? PMID Step 3   35

    Chapter 5: What Did You feel? PMID Step 4   46

    Chapter 6: What Should You Do? PMID Step 5   55

    Chapter 7: Who's in Your Dream? PMID Step 6   62

Contents - 2

SECTION	PAGE

Section C: Series of Relationship Dreams   74

    Chapter 8:   Dreams about Parents   77
                          Alice's Dream about Dad (more)   78
                          William's Dream about Father   93
                          Eleanor's Dream about Mama   99

    Chapter 9:   Coincidence of Psi-dreams of Marital Pair: Same Night Dreams   114

    Chapter 10:   Galen's Dream Snatches about Victorious Handling of Situations   117

Section D: **Other Type Dreams, and Putting it all Together**   **122**

    Chapter 11:   Facing Nightmares and Scary Dreams, Facing Life   123

    Chapter 12:   Everyday Dreams, Everyday Life   131

    Chapter 13:   Spiritual Dreams, Spiritual Life   143

    Chapter 14:   Lucid Dreams, Living Dreams   156

    Chapter 15:   Living Dreams, Living Life, Putting it all together   160

Contents - 3

SECTION	PAGE
Epilogue	**164**
Table: Personalized Method for Interpreting Dreams	166
Appendices:	
Appendix 1: Dream Phrase Directory (and Symbols)	167
Appendix 2: Research and Explorations of the Personalized Method for Interpreting Dreams (PMID), including assessment instruments used	172
Appendix 3: About the International Organization for the Study of Dreams	183
Appendix 4: Suggested Exercises for Chapters 1 through 15	184
Appendix 5: Historical Perspectives and Some Contemporary Dream Interpretation Models	187
Bibliography	**197**

Acknowledgements

John Duesbury's (my husband) quiet zeal and ingenious style together with his ability to intensely support another's projects although they may differ from his own immediate ventures, was invaluable to my ability to complete the work of this book.

Steven Duesbury's (our son) encouragement to follow my own dreams was of great effect in my doing just that, literally and figuratively. And thanks, thanks, thanks, Steven, for rewriting *Living Dreams, Living Life*. It came to life after you rewrote major portions of this book into common layperson's language.

Deep appreciation to the University of Wisconsin-Whitewater Counselor Education and Distance Education departments, with special thanks to David Van Doren, Ed. D. for his encouragement to research the PMID model beyond the thesis. Also special thanks to Anene Okocha, Ph.D., Brenda O'Beirne, Ph.D., and Don Norman, Ph. D. for their guidance and continuing support.

Thanks to James King, Ph.D., and Kimberly Tuescher, Ph.D., University of Wisconsin-Platteville for generous professional assistance. Appreciative recognition to the University of Wisconsin-Platteville Karrmann Interlibrary staff for providing reference materials during our research and exploration projects.

My dream of a quiet Black man with an unshaven beard led to Dr. Edward Bruce Bynum being consultant to me. The value of his encouragement, clinical expertise, and friendship is truly a dream come true. Two of Dr. Bynum's books are *Families and the Interpretation of Dreams* and *The African Unconscious*.

We recognize and appreciate the International Association for the Study of Dreams, its members, professionals, counselors, therapists, artists and its worldwide community of dreamers for their intellectual and scholarly support on so many levels.

Ethics Statement

We celebrate the many benefits of dreamwork, yet we recognize that there are potential risks. We agree with the ethical position taken by the International Association for the Study of Dreams (www.asdreams.org), in that we support an approach to dreamwork and dream sharing that respects the dreamer's dignity and integrity, and that recognizes the dreamer as the decision-maker regarding the significance of the dream. Systems of dreamwork that assign authority or knowledge of the dream's meanings to someone other than the dreamer can be misleading, incorrect, and harmful. Ethical dreamwork helps the dreamer work with his/her own dream images, feelings, and associations, and guides the dreamer to experience, appreciate, and understand the dream more fully.

A dreamer's decision to share or discontinue sharing a dream should always be respected and honored. The dreamer should be forewarned that unexpected issues or emotions might arise in the course of the dreamwork. Information and mutual agreement about the degree of privacy and confidentiality are essential ingredients in creating a safe atmosphere for dream sharing.

Dreamwork outside a clinical setting is not a substitute for professional counseling or other professional treatment, and should not be used as such.

(Adapted from International Association
for the Study of Dreams Prototype)

Section A: Introductory

Introduction to *Living Dreams, Living Life*

How *should* you live your life?
How do you *want* to live your life?

These questions are very different and far from rhetorical. In fact, confusion about these questions has reached a crisis point in America and much of the westernized world.

As we have become more modern and prosperous as a culture, we have increasingly lost our way as individual people. Reports of depression rates and sales of pharmaceuticals to relieve our pain are at record levels.

More specifically, we wonder how we can live more fully and experience more happiness, fulfillment and contentment in our lives. In short, we want to know how to live our dreams.

It's a question all people ask themselves throughout their lives. And not only are the answers sometimes frustratingly difficult to find, they also keep changing.

What works for us as children is obviously different as we reach young adulthood. Even after marriage, family, career and other life "milestones" of being an adult have been achieved, the question keeps coming back and the answer keeps changing.

We are all clearly asking questions, but precious few are finding answers. This results in unnecessary frustration and sadness and, in some cases, a seemingly permanent sense of failure and emptiness.

We have literally and figuratively forgotten our dreams and, in the process, lost touch with our lives and ourselves.

But our literal dreams can provide the single most useful and effective way to rediscover our figurative dreams, the lives we truly want to live and the people we truly want to be.

Before we get into how dream interpretation can provide an unparalleled method to living our lives to the fullest, it's important first to take a couple of steps back and understand exactly what the problem is, how and why we arrived at this point, and in what ways the basic question of "why dreams" can be the key to resolving these issues.

To truly live our lives to the fullest it's important first to understand the basic problem that leads to our disappointment, frustration and general confusion in our lives.

Whose life are you living?

Are you living the life you think you *should* be living, or are you fully living your life in the way that you *want* to live it?

It's a deceptively tricky question that has been at the core of spiritual, philosophical, psychological and dream study for centuries. In more modern times, it remains the basic question that therapists had worked to help their patients answer even before the days of Freud and Jung.

The question of personal happiness and life satisfaction often comes down to resolving a basic gap between what we experience in our conscious minds (all the *shoulds* of our waking minds) and what lives and swims in our unconscious minds (our true beliefs and uncensored desires).

Successfully navigating and integrating these two realms gives you a strong sense of purpose, joy, self-satisfaction and contentment. The greater the connection between your conscious and unconscious, the greater will be your positive experience of yourself and your life.

Failure to balance these elements successfully leads to feelings of frustration, confusion, anger, depression and a general sense of feeling stuck or possibly adrift with no strong direction or purpose in life. The greater disconnect between the two, the more pronounced these feelings become.

Some people may also experience flip-flops between sometimes living primarily in their own little fantasy worlds to other times being immersed entirely in the real world with little or no experience of their own emotions. In extreme cases, an individual can lose touch with this "reality" and, in the process, miss the greater reality altogether.

The question of "whose life are you living?" is deceptively tricky because it's often easy really not to know. Sometimes it's hard to know just what we *do* want in our lives, let alone figure out how to achieve it.

How can it be so difficult just to know what kind of life we really want?

This begs the question of where all this confusion came from in the first place. If the key is simply keeping our conscious and unconscious minds connected, then how and why did we ever stop doing it?

You against the world

Albeit somewhat overstated, the fact remains that from your first breath your life has hinged on the struggle between your needs and desires and those of the people, organizations, and culture that surround you.

This is not to say that every moment of your life is a hard fought struggle for survival. Our own personal experience shows this not to be true at all. However, it is a personal struggle that you face daily in which your defeat can ultimately lead to a loss of your self.

The reason for this struggle is obvious and necessary. We can't all run around rampantly and selfishly satisfying our own needs and desires whenever and however we please. We can't just beat up somebody on the street who annoys us any more than we can just start having sex with anybody whom we find attractive, no matter how strong or how aware we are of our deeper desires.

And as we examine our development from infant to adulthood we can see how we've slowly learned to inhibit ourselves in order to assimilate and function in an ever-broadening world both to our own personal benefit and detriment.

As infants our whole life (and most everyone else's around us) centered on our personal satisfaction. From our perspective, the whole universe revolved around our need for food, sleep, and, even when we poop.

As we grew, we learned that we must restrict ourselves in order to fit into systems beyond our physical self, the first of which was our own family. We learned delayed gratification -- that even if we were hungry, we had to wait until mealtime. We learned to control ourselves physically through the significant step of toilet training. We learned that we could not make whatever sounds we wanted whenever and wherever we wanted.

As we matured further, we continued to learn to restrict ourselves to fit into larger and more complex systems. We adapted to schedules, classrooms and other sets of rules as we entered school. We also learned to do more things (such as homework or helping around the house) based on requests or expectations of others, primarily those in authority.

Our own needs also became much more elaborate and more difficult to satisfy. We found that just wanting to play a game wasn't enough if our skills weren't good enough to be picked for a team or play the position we wanted. We discovered that some people didn't like us and others could be downright mean and purposely hurtful.

Still further, as we reached our teens we began our struggle for independence and self-discovery in earnest, while at the same time the pressures for conformity and acceptance sometimes became all encompassing.

Even the most average of academic students become well-versed students in the school of life, continually being educated and reinforced by waves of mass media, advertising, rock stars, movies, famous athletes, and the celebration and imitation of these by their peers (especially the cool ones).

The deep fears of being labeled "uncool," no matter how contrived or inane the definition or demands, could often lead to extreme behaviors based solely on external expectations. In other cases, some teens rebel, purposely seeking adamantly not to fit, but always with keen awareness of a rebellion against the status quo.

By graduation from high school, most folks achieve an advanced degree in the knowledge of "normal" and the related expectations as taught by parents, authority figures and society-at-large. In short, many of people discover they have defined themselves almost entirely by external criteria and values.

Yet, they had barely begun their own discovery of self or sense of personal values and criteria, long ago burying the narcissistic inner child deep inside and out of sight from public ridicule. People have precious few years' experience or knowledge of adult emotions or sexuality, with only a confused grasp of mature love based on moments of thumping hearts and back seat groupings. High school graduates had yet even to make a first real step out into the world on their own.

This is not to say the culturalization and some level of assimilation are wrong and not necessary both for society as a whole and for an individual's well-being. The very ability to develop and maintain mature relationships hinges on these learned skills.

The point of this brief review of human development is to help us realize that people -- all of us were educated much earlier and more intensely in the *shoulds* of our lives than about our own selves. The discovery of choosing how we want to live for our own satisfaction and fulfillment in a healthy balance with these other social and cultural needs is, indeed, the dance of a happy life.

This makes clear why the question of "Whose life are you living?" can be so difficult. We have been encouraged at times to over emphasize the external and the conscious self to the great harm and loss of our internal selves. Even when we recognize that we may be living our lives for others, it still doesn't help us answer what kind of life *we* really want to live.

Finding *your* answers for *your* life

Given our understanding of how and why we face the confusion we do, it's now more obvious than ever why it's so critical to pay attention to the bias and agenda of any resource we turn to for answers.

And, the fact is, with the exception of highly skilled counselors, any person, organization or resource you find will bring some level of self-serving bias or agenda.

Some are very obvious, such as TV shows that seek higher ratings and, in turn, higher advertising dollars. This is true for all media. Their priority is drawing the greatest numbers of viewers, readers or listeners with information that creates the broadest appeal for the greatest number of people, not in providing the most balanced, factual advice.

We are all very aware of this, yet we pick up the latest fashion magazine to get advice for the best diets. We fully understand that the snippets we see of celebrities' lives don't offer a full or at all real picture, yet we feel that we've somehow fallen short in our lives because we don't measure up to them. It's obvious to all of us that a TV personality has no specific knowledge of our own personal problems or even that we exist to them, yet the person's fame and mass appeal leads us to expect that they really must know what they're talking about, so we'd better pay attention.

Advertising is especially insidious in this regard because of its constant attempts to create a personal connection with potential buyers. Tremendous amounts of demographic and psychodynamic research go into creating a sense of need that can best be satisfied by purchasing a product or service.

Again, we are all very aware of this, yet the sheer volume of messages convinces us that maybe we really aren't up to par in various ways.

A loving Christian church no matter how inclusive and open-minded is unlikely to tell you to leave the flock and become a Buddhist. A spouse in love with you can hardly be expected to tell you that leaving the relationship is the healthiest path for you. A friend may encourage you not to pursue an out-of-state job opportunity because it could lead to the loss of your relationship.

This is not to say that there is anything necessarily insidious about these agendas. Many times those closest to us aren't fully aware of their own biases and may give us self-serving advice even with the best intentions and desires to care for our welfare.

Even counselors bring their own biases, but the key difference here is that they are trained in the recognition of transference and counter transference dynamics. Thus, they are aware of this process and, thereby, constantly strive to be on guard against putting their personal feelings before a patient's. This is a constant struggle for even the best-trained counselors.

Even so, the pure objective of therapy or counseling is to help the client reconnect with his or her *own* true feelings, desires, wants and needs. The role of the counselor is to provide *unbiased* support and guidance to help facilitate the client's self-discovery and self-understanding.

Contrary to some beliefs, good counselors do not tell you what to do or how you should feel. One most ironic thing about counseling is that whereas most clients come in wanting to be told the answers to their life problems, they often already have the answers they're looking for buried deep inside themselves.

The second key role for therapy is helping clients integrate this self-knowledge and understanding into their everyday lives. Obviously, it does no good just to realize that you have a drinking problem if you're going to keep going out drinking every night. A counselor can help you discover ways (many times very obvious) that you can change, manage or even discontinue this behavior based on whatever is healthiest for you.

Note that unbiased and non-judgmental discussions are paramount. The more trusting and open the relationship between client and counselor, the more successful the work. And, short of criminal behavior or actions that could result in severe physical harm to yourself or others, a good counselor avoids determining good or bad behaviors for you. Those are subjective terms that can only be defined by the clients based on their own personal emotions and perspectives.

In essence helping *you* find *your* answers to *your* life is the whole basis and practice of good counseling and psychotherapy. It is, therefore, no surprise that it is also the whole basis and practice of dream interpretation.

Living Your Dreams

The answer to our question earlier in the chapter of "why dreams" should now be clear. The study and understanding of your dreams provides you with the ability to reconnect with your *deeper self -- your all-important unconscious* -- to rediscover your deepest personal emotions and desires for yourself and your life.

Dreams do much more than provide insights into your deepest feelings. Knowing these feelings is just the first step. As we've discussed, the *real key is to reconnect your unconscious emotions with your waking life.*

The final piece of this puzzle, and the greatest value of what we'll teach you about working with your dreams, is that dreams provide tremendous insights about your waking life actions and suggestions for what you can do to realize your dreams, literally and figuratively.

What's more, this is not something that necessarily requires months or years of training and practice.

In fact, the Personalized Method for Interpreting Dreams (PMID) we will explain in the following pages was created specifically to provide anyone -- even those with little or no dreamwork experience -- with the greatest understanding of their dreams as quickly as possible.

We are continually amazed how often even the most inexperienced of people almost immediately make startling connections and discoveries that have profound impact on their lives by simply using the techniques explained in the following pages. The following story is just one example.

Carol's Story: Opening Up to the world

(We note upfront that Carol's only experience in dreamwork was a general understanding of the PMID process gained through various casual discussions with us. She had received no formal training, nor had even discussed the PMID process at any great length with us.)

Carol, a business associate of ours, is an attractive 42-year-old woman who was reared in a somewhat conservative and traditional Christian household. She and her husband have been happily married for 15 years, with no kids, and both are owners of successful businesses. They enjoy spending time sailing on their boat and traveling to far-flung destinations on SCUBA diving trips, a passion of theirs for years.

Somewhat shy and reserved at first meeting, Carol is very intelligent and self-assured, quite witty, and enjoys the company of a wide variety of close friends.

By all standards and appearances, Carol has a very wonderful life, an assessment with which she readily agrees.

Carol had also occasionally mentioned that she was feeling somewhat confused. It appeared that it was of little concern for her, and as was her style, she didn't really express specifically why and was somewhat reticent to discuss the matter in any depth.

Then, during a recent dinner with her, she surprised us by bringing up her "confusion" again. Once again, she was hesitant to discuss the matter, but did share two additional insights. One, although she wasn't sure what the confusion was about, she just knew (prefaced with the usual "this is going to sound stupid") that she wanted to feel "bigger." By "bigger" she explained that she wanted to feel more alive or more . . . something.

Her other disclosure was that there was a great deal about herself that she always kept secret from everybody, including her husband. She explained the reason was not due to these secrets being so awful or shameful, but that she just felt uncomfortable disclosing intimate things about herself. She even commented that on the few occasions she had opened up a bit more, she often felt strong guilt the next day for being so personal, statements that surprised us given our personal experience with her.

Given what she had shared, we called her the next morning to reassure her about her disclosures, however minor they may have seemed, and make sure she wasn't feeling any guilt over the conversation. To our pleasant surprise Carol greeted us with an extremely cheery, "Did you read my email?" which we had not yet done.

She then excitedly told us about a dream she had had following our dinner discussion. In fact, she had awakened to this dream even though she reported rarely even remembering dreams.

Her dream had been quite brief, and her memory of it rather vague. But one part stuck out clearly for her. As Carol described it to us:

I was upstairs in my house, and had heard people downstairs. When I went downstairs to investigate, I found my living room filled with strangers, but I was oddly not scared at all and knew they meant no harm.

I wondered how they had gotten in, so I went to the front door to see if it was locked. But when I looked at the door I discovered that not only was the door not locked, it didn't even have a lock or any kind of latch or doorknob either!

"Don't you get it?" she asked us in a surprisingly enthusiastic voice. "The door . . . *my* door, wasn't locked anymore. It was open so people could come in. And that's okay. It's okay to let people in sometimes!" She was thrilled, and so were we.

"I'm sure there's a lot more to my dream," Carol continued. "And I'd like to learn about that sometime, but I'm just really excited about that door. I feel great!"

As we noted earlier, Carol's experience was certainly very significant, but not at all unusual. Her experience was a perfect example of how a dream, even a simple door in a dream, can bring deeper insights about one's self and open one's eyes to a new perspective in the waking life that literally opens new doors, as in Carol's case.

Like anything, the more you learn about working with your dreams, and the more you practice the teachings in this book, the richer and more profound your experiences will be.

But simply deciphering every part of a dream is not the end goal. As in Carol's case, the true value of understanding dreams is to see those critical connections between your dreams and your waking life experiences in order to enhance your daily life.

Simply put, when you start living the lessons of your dreams, you will start living the life that you dream.

Chapter 1

The Personalized Method for Interpreting Dreams (PMID)– Preliminary Work

Getting started

The single biggest challenge most people face when first working with their dreams is also the most obvious: simply remembering dreams. Obviously, it's pretty hard to understand the message of a dream that cannot be recalled.

Many people we work with will initially tell us that they don't remember any of their dreams. Whereas this may be factually accurate, it is also technically misleading.

In truth, the reason people don't remember their dreams, is they've just forgotten how. As very young children, our dreams were sometimes as real and vivid as our waking life. As we matured, many of us started to pay less and less attention to our dreams, in the process teaching ourselves not to remember dreams.

In a sense, most people have spent every night of their entire adult lives practicing *not* to remember their dreams, in much the same way that someone who lives in a big city often doesn't even hear the many sirens going by daily. Is it any wonder that they now don't automatically remember them?

So, the first step in helping you to remember your dreams is simply to start *trying* to remember them. And, this can be surprisingly easy to do. This may sound almost too easy to be true for some. Yet, this simple step can be amazingly effective.

The other change we see is that often after people have some initial successes in remembering a few dreams, they begin remembering more and more dreams. This makes sense, since dreaming is a natural behavior and, therefore, dream recall could come easily once we are open to it.

We provide the following list of some of the easiest and most effective things you can do to improve your dream recall.

Dream recall

- Tell yourself before you go to sleep that you will recall your dreams. It is often best simply to prompt dream recall by telling yourself before you go to sleep, "I will remember a dream when I wake up," instead of asking for answers to detailed questions. Then your dreaming mind will be more likely to respond to your emotional needs as perceived by your inner nature than to your cognitive directions.
- When you wake, lie very still, remain in a relaxed, almost drowsy state, and wait for dream recall to emerge into your mind.
- If no recall comes after you have been lying very still for a while, try turning slowly from one position to another and wait for recall.
- When you have recall, while continuing to lie still, rehearse the dream(s) in your mind.
- Keep a pad and pencil near your bed, or keep a tape recorder near your bed and write the dream down (or voice record it if you prefer) as soon as you wake.
- Be alert for dream recall during the day, especially during relaxed times.
- Trust the process. Be confident in your ability to recall dreams. Remember, all people dream as a matter of biological necessity. It is the recall or conscious memory of the dream that can be difficult at times.

How to record your dream

There are a couple of tips to keep in mind that will help you both (1) to recall the dream in greater detail and (2) to record the dream in a way that will be easiest for you to understand and interpret.

Record your dreams in the first person and present tense to foster the immediate and intimate feelings of the dream. Include your dreaming emotions in the dream narrative itself, since emotions are integral parts of the dreaming experience. Record every recalled detail of the dream, regardless of its seeming relatedness or importance. Often seeming insignificant details are keys to developing dream meanings later. As a member of www.yourguidingdreams.com remarked, "I often am astonished at the clarity of connections that comes from writing the dream down."

Retain the dream script as originally written. Dreams contain suggestions for improving the dreamer's circumstances. If we change the dream to fit our derived meanings, we might distort the dream's helpful suggestions.

Also, remember that a dream doesn't have to be overly long or complex to have a deep meaning for you, as we saw from Carol's dream in our Introduction. Hers was a simple dream about a door that opened her eyes to some very exciting new opportunities in her life.

As a final step, before we jump into learning to interpret your dreams, we first want to give you a brief overview of *how* you'll learn to understand your dreams through the PMID model and, equally important, *why* the PMID process is so effective in going beyond simple dream interpretation to give you a deeper understanding of how you can change your life.

Overview of the Personalized Method for Interpreting Dreams (PMID)

The PMID process has been developed during more than a decade and has been tested and refined through work with clinicians and graduate students. While shown beneficial for professional use, early in the development of the PMID process we discovered an extremely underserved group of people who could generally be described as having little or no current interest in seeing a counseling professional but were very interested in their own personal growth and happiness -- people in the general population. We then researched the general population's ability to use the PMID model; see results included in Appendix 2 Research and Explorations of the Personalized Method for Interpreting Dreams (PMID).

In Section B, we will explore the PMID process in greater depth and demonstrate how the steps build on each other with an actual dream interpretation conducted with an associate. For now, as a brief overview, the PMID process has six basic steps. Concisely stated, those steps are:

Step 1: Day-before-dream **event(s)** that connects to this dream.
Step 2: Day-before-dream **thought(s)** that connects to this dream.
Step 3: **Major dream phrases** (and symbols) defined in the context of this dream.
Step 4: Dreaming **emotions** compared with waking life emotions about issue in this dream.
Step 5: **Solutions or suggestions** for changing thoughts, attitudes or behaviors (answer[s] to day-before-my-dream thoughts).
Step 6: Dreaming and waking life **reactions** to each person in this dream.

The full PMID steps are presented step by step within Chapters 2, 3, 4, 5, 6, and 7, and are also presented in one table after the Epilogue to this book.

It's not important that you memorize or even fully understand exactly what each step entails at this point. What's important here is to see the process as a whole and to recognize some key points:

- Each step in the process strongly emphasizes connections between your dream and your waking life. This is critical to gain an understanding of your dream in a way that provides practical value and answers for your waking life.
- Your *personal* meanings for the dream (especially in exploring meanings to dream phrases and symbols in Step 3) are what are most critical and beneficial to you -- and not worrying about getting the "right" interpretation. As you'll soon learn, *your* interpretation is most times the "right" one, and you'll know it better than anyone else.
- Relationships are vital to our waking lives and, so, naturally, are keys to understanding our dreams (as in Step 6). This step is rarely -- if ever -- included in most dream analysis, which leads to much invaluable information in dreams being ignored, just as would happen in our waking lives if we didn't consider the role of our relationships in our lives.

Each step builds incrementally upon those before it. Step 1 clarifies what waking life issue your dream is about. Step 2 captures question(s) that your dream answers. Based on that, we are much better able to understand the symbolism (Step 3), recognize our deeper emotions surrounding the issue (Step 4), discover what we should do to solve the problem (Step 5), and clearly understand the roles our most important relationships play in the situation (Step 6).

Aside from modifying the language of the PMID process so as not to be overly technical and more easily used by those with little or no dream work experience, the process you're about to learn is the same process we developed during our research. (See Appendix 2 for Research and Explorations of the Personalized Method for Interpreting Dreams)

We've included a number of sample dreams in Sections C and D to help you become familiar with some of the endless ways the PMID process works in helping you to understand your dreams.

However, **we strongly suggest** that you first read through Section B, which provides the important detailed explanations and examples for learning before skipping farther ahead in the book. As we've said, none of these steps, or the PMID process itself, is difficult or complex. It is specifically designed to be anything but. Still, the more you learn in the following Section B, the more you'll benefit from the example dreams in the back.

To this point, we've talked a lot *about* dreaming dreams and their role in our lives. It's time to start *doing* . . . and dreaming.

Section B

Living Dreams, Finding Answers with the PMID Model

Introduction to Section B

Our purpose in this Section is to show you how to use the Personalized Method for Interpreting Dreams (PMID) to interpret your dreams. With the PMID dream interpretation model the dreamer interprets her or his dreams. When a counselor is involved, the dreamer is still the interpreter; the counselor facilitates the process.

Relationship dreams are our focus in Sections A, B, and C of this book. Other types of dreams are our focus in Section D. Because dreams reflect emotional concerns and the majority of our emotional concerns are with personal relationships, dreamwork approaches to personal relationship issues can be immensely helpful.

Further, a dreamwork *systems* approach can be immensely helpful. Are you familiar with family systems perspectives of counseling? From a family systems perspective, each member of a family affects and is affected by other family members to the extent it makes no sense to attempt to understand the individual in isolation. In family counseling models, the family meets with a counselor or therapist to alleviate concerns about relationships. With a *dreamwork* systems approach, instead of having the family together in a counseling session, the individual, either alone or facilitated by a counselor, studies dreams about major relationships in his or her life to understand self and alleviate stress.

We demonstrate the PMID model in Section B with a dream about the dreamer's dad and her interpretations of it. The dream is shown next.
Note: Dreamer's words (Dream and PMID steps) are in italics.

The Dream–

Dad and the Inventory (Dreamer is Alice)

During the first part of my dream a young woman friend, Tara, has left her children in another part of the world where she and her family are vacationing, and she is back home by herself to make an inventory of all of her furniture. I am very surprised that she leaves her children. She asks me if I have made an inventory of everything in our house. Later I hear old tapes playing her voice saying suspicious things about us, and I am shocked about that, having no idea she had suspicions about our doings.

I'm then in a new scene -- we are outside in front of our house (I somehow know it's my house, but it doesn't look familiar). I am sitting on the edge of what seems to be a flowerbed, but the yard is untended. It has lots of bare places. I think about it and think how it used to be green, and it surely seems like we kept up taking care of it and mowed it.

Thomas is sitting at the front of the lawn area toward the road. There is what seems to be a pile of junk or perhaps junk items beside my husband. Suddenly something comes out of the pile. It is someone covered up with a canvas or tarp -- like a sack over his head. My husband talks to it a bit it seems -- but it is for me.

The covered figure comes back where I am and suddenly the sack is gone. Now I see that the figure is my dad, who passed away years ago. I think that I must be dreaming, but I really want to talk with my dad.

My dad's eyes -- around his eyes are red -- it is like the flesh around his eyes is pulled out or enlarged just a little and it is red. His expression is one of emotion -- like he has been worn weary with emotion.

I want to say to him how I'm so glad he came to get this worked out. I keep thinking how to say it to him to get it right. I don't want really to accuse him, it seems -- but just to get this rage worked out . . . the rage related to being falsely accused without being allowed to defend myself or he would call my anger proof of my guilt.

I just get started talking and my dad turns into what appears to be a heavy barked tree. I first can see his facial features like a somewhat heavy outline of bark protruding from the trunk of the tree. And then his features slowly fade into the bark of the tree -- and I don't see him anymore. I plead some with him to stay so we can get this cleared up.

Thomas says something to me -- like wanting me not to pursue this -- but I'm very upset that Thomas wants to stop the dream and I tell him, "Don't wake me. My dad is here and I want to get this cleared up" -- to that effect.

The scene changes and I am standing out at the top of the driveway hill at my parents' farm implement business. It takes me a little bit to realize that this is where I am. I am still aware I am dreaming. The sun is shining.

I talk to Dad, although I don't see him. I say, "Dad, look, this is the implement business buildings and our house." I look at the house. I seem to talk to him as I see each thing. "They are working on the house. Oh, they are painting the house. They are painting it gray. There is an area between the top and bottom of the house that isn't painted."

I see that all the other buildings are painted gray. They are in fine repair, though. They all look fine, but they are painted gray. I don't ask why the color is gray or think to ask why the gray color in the dream. I am merely observing.

Chapter 2

What's Happening In Your Life? PMID Step 1

Dreams reach to the peripheries of the mind -- further than waking thought usually ever goes.

Upon waking and asking themselves, "What did that dream mean?" many peoples' first reaction is to start exploring all the symbolism in an effort to find some answers.

In fact, the easiest (and best) place to start looking for the true meaning of your dreams is in your own waking life. Attempts to first start trying to decipher the symbolism of dreams can often be misleading and downright frustrating.

Dreams reach to the peripheries of the mind -- further than waking thought usually ever goes. It's not surprising that your dreaming language is often somewhat more difficult to understand than your waking life language, especially at first. So, you will need a little help. The first step is to connect your dream to something that happened to you before you had the dream.

> **PMID Step 1:** Record the **event(s)** you had before your dream (most often, day before) that appear either objectively or figuratively in this dream.

Synesius of Cyrene, North African scholar and philosopher who lived about 365-414 AD, encouraged people to record their waking life experiences along with their dreams to help them make connections between their waking life events and their dreams.[1]

With the PMID model, the major emphasis is on paying attention to how what happened in the day or evening before the dream ties to the dream content.[2] Often what happens in the dreamer's waking life the day before the dream concerns relationship experiences. Ernest Hartmann, M.D. said that dreams "often seem to be dealing with interpersonal problems, with the dreamer's current concerns about family, friends, lovers" and dreams "appear to make connections with other persons or experiences in the past. ..."[3] Hartmann also notes there is "little question that . . . we appear to make distant connections or associations more easily during dreaming than during waking thought."[4]

Given how busy peoples' lives are, it's clearly very difficult to make any kind of detailed list of all of one's activities. Nor is it necessary or even very helpful to do so. The major events in your life that come quickly to mind are those that you are most likely to dream about.

So, it's helpful to just ask yourself a couple of easy questions:

1. **What did I do the day before the dream?** Just remind yourself about what you were doing and what happened during the day. An award? An unkind remark? A phone call from a friend?
2. **Are there any significant ongoing issues in your life?** Again, a detailed list isn't necessary. An upcoming social event? A desire to lose weight? Some difficulty with your spouse? Did something happen yesterday that involved any of these?

---

[1] Synesius of Cyrene. (excerpts cited in Kelsey, *God, Dreams, and Revelation.* Minneapolis, MN, 1991, p. 251.)

[2] E. Duesbury. "Personalized Method for Interpreting Dreams (PMID) -- As applied to relationship issues," *Dreaming: Journal of the Association for the Study of Dreams,* 11(4), 2001, pp. 207-216; E. Duesbury. Utilizing Dreams to Understand and Mollify Relationship Issues. University of Wisconsin-Whitewater, 2000.

[3] E. Hartmann. "Making Connections in a Safe Place: Is Dreaming Psychotherapy?" *Dreaming, Journal of the Association for the Study of Dreams* 5(4), 1995, pp. 213-228.

[4] E. Hartmann. "Making Connections in a Safe Place: Is Dreaming Psychotherapy?" *Dreaming, Journal of the Association for the Study of Dreams* 5(4), 1995, pp. 213-228.

Record the previous day's events after waking from your dream because it is after the dream that connections to specific event(s) can be made. Record these the same time you record your dream or as they occur to you during the day or evening.

As an alternative, before going to sleep each night, record the day's events in a journal. This alternative practice may be beneficial for beginners and for people who have difficulty making connections after the dream.

Applying Step 1

Now, let's take a look back at events that lead up to our dream and see if there are any connections. The connections Alice, the dreamer, made to her "Inventory" dream are:

- *The day before this dream, I read a book that suggested ways to help identify and release anger. One of the techniques suggested in the book was an inventorying exercise in which you relax. Then you think of the person you are angry with and then just watch what thoughts come into your mind about that person. I was attracted to the thought inventorying exercise the author suggested and began doing the exercise, using my dad as the possible person toward whom I was unconsciously harboring anger.*
- *The night before the dream, I prayed for release from any possible latent anger feelings toward Dad.*

Some of Alice's other prominent events from the day and evening before this dream were:

- *I skipped cleaning my eyeglass lenses last night, but nearly always clean the lenses on Tuesday evenings.*
- *I called the library for resources on functioning of the human eyes.*
- *A cement truck backed out in the way of oncoming traffic just as I was driving out, and I couldn't see around it. A neighbor came running over to help.*
- *I wrote a letter to a friend with a suggestion my husband had for him.*
- *I did laundry.*

If your dreams do not seem to connect to your previous day(s) events and circumstances, don't become discouraged. Give your best efforts to recording your previous day's events and circumstances and you will gradually be able to make connections.

Even when you are unable to make connections at the time of your dream, it is very important to record pre-dream events and circumstances at the time of your dream. Otherwise, you will lose these important clues for when you revisit your dream for new insights.

Ongoing significant issues provide background that could be useful to understand dreams. Ongoing issues for Alice at this time included:

- *Spiritual pursuits*
- *Work on reducing stress from relationship concerns*

Now, when we look back at the dream, some interesting connections start becoming very apparent.

PMID Step 1 Day before the dream **event** connections to Alice's Dream

First, you'll recall that at the beginning of Alice's dream (see the dream, "Dad and the Inventory," near beginning of Section B) a young woman friend, Tara, was busy making an inventory of all of her furniture -- making a list of everything in her house just as Alice had been doing when she inventoried her thoughts about her dad the day before her dream.

We can immediately start to see our first big clue to understanding the dream -- the *theme* of her dream: **a desire to bring to light and address any unresolved feelings of anger toward my dad.**

That clue comes from Alice simply connecting her waking life "inventory" exercise with the "inventory" in the dream that the neighbor Tara was so concerned about doing, even asking Alice if she had done it yet! There is also the obvious connection between the dream and Alice saying her prayers before going to sleep. Her prayers connect clearly with the appearance of her dad in the dream and to the physical setting for much of the dream (the house and buildings where Alice was reared).

The *theme* of the dream provides an important basis and context for understanding everything else that happens. Often it will be apparent in obvious connections early in your dream, such as the connection with inventory in this dream.

> **Dream Themes**
>
> To help you further connect events to dreams, here are some more examples (associated dreams not included in this writing) of events that set the themes for the subsequent dreams:
>
> - **Somewhat subtle connection:** You have an intense discussion with your mom. That night you dream of a many-leveled house containing items on each floor that remind you of your mom.
> - **More subjective (figurative):** The day before your dream you attend a social event at which people visited with you about highly political matters, and you did quite well in remaining calm, which is unlike your usual response. Your usual response is to become hyperactive in such conversations. That night you dream that a cousin (hyperactive family member) has died -- though in waking life, he is still alive. Your hyperactivity has diminished -- died.
> - **Obscure connection:** The day before your dream, your supervisor calls you into her office and reprimands you. While you are in her office, you notice a porcelain doll. That night you dream about a porcelain doll -- your supervisor is not in your dream. Although the porcelain doll connects to your dream, the doll likely is only a prompter for your dream; the important connection, theme, or category of your dream is your reaction to your supervisor's reprimand. The porcelain doll just makes you aware of the actual theme of the dream.

So, now we've got a solid understanding of what the dream is generally about, but what of all the other things in it, such as Alice's dad turning into a tree? And why is her husband in it? What's the deal with the unpainted strip and the gray buildings? Those seemed to have nothing to do with anything.

Even more, what is Alice supposed to learn from the dream? That she's still mad at her dad? That he's still mad at her? That he's been reincarnated as a tree? (One would hope not.) Maybe Alice is supposed to make a list of everything in her house, as Tara said in the dream.

The answers lie in digging a little deeper, going beyond the events of our lives and deeper into our thoughts as we will discover in the next chapter.

Chapter 3

What's on Your Mind? PMID Step 2

In this chapter, we are going to move to a deeper connectivity between our dreams and our daily life. As we learned in the last chapter, first recalling the most recent (often the day or evening before your dream) events in your life provides both an easy way to learn what your dream is generally about (the theme) and to help see how your dream connects to your waking life.

PMID Step 1 provides the context of "what" your dream is about. In our example, we learned that the theme of the dream is Alice's desire to bring to light and address any unresolved feelings of anger toward her dad. This is obviously a critical first step before digging deeper into specific meanings of the dream in the same way that if someone just says, "tree" to you, it doesn't really tell you much. You need the context of what tree they're talking about, why the tree is significant (Is it beautiful or going to fall on me?) to make sense of the word "tree."

The next step of PMID Step 2 is to connect our pre-dream thoughts (most often, day before going to sleep and dreaming) to our dream contents by treating the dream as a responsive answer to our pre-dream thoughts. PMID Step 2 digs deeper into the question of why you had this dream and what the dream is telling you about the subject of the dream.

> **PMID Step 2:** Record the **thought(s)** you had before your dream (most often, day before) that seem to connect to this dream either objectively or figuratively. Write "I thought" statements to help clarify which pre-dream thought(s) brought this dream.

Dream researchers have long recognized that thoughts passing through our waking minds are tremendous initiators of dreams.[5] In the PMID process, we treat thoughts as questions that the dream responds to or answers. The dreamer is able to identify the question(s) that the dream answers by connecting previous day(s) thoughts to the dream. When the dreamer does not connect day-before thoughts to the dream, it is like having the answer to a question without knowing the question.[6]

Hildebrant (in his 1875 book on dreams) claimed it would be possible to explain every dream image if enough time were available to trace it to its origin in the "chambers of one's memory." He said, "It is impossible to think of any action in a dream for which the original motive was not in some way or other -- whether as a wish, or desire or impulse -- passed through the waking mind."[7]

Repeatedly, we find that thoughts trigger emotions into stressful feelings. That awareness makes us acutely conscious of thoughts as keys to dream interpretation. We, the dreamers, must notice our thoughts and take full responsibility for the results of their intensity. Dreams not only help us notice our thoughts and emotions, but they also reveal sources and intensity of thoughts and emotions.

Thoughts that initiate dreams are very often about the events that occurred the day before our dreams. PMID Step 2 requires us to notice what was really important to us from our list of events in PMID Step 1.

We all experience numerous big and small events throughout the day. What's critical is noticing those events that are important to us. Your list of events in PMID Step 1 could include a call from your child's teacher, getting cut off in traffic, or spilling coffee on yourself.

---

[5] M. Kramer, T. Roth, D. Arand, & M. Bonnet. "Waking and Dreaming Mentation: A Test of Their Interrelationship," *Neuroscience Letters 22*, 1981, pp. 83-86.

[6] E. Duesbury. "Personalized Method for Interpreting Dreams (PMID) -- As applied to relationship issues," *Dreaming: Journal of the Association for the Study of Dreams,* 11(4), 2001, 207-216; E. Duesbury. Utilizing Dreams to Understand and Mollify Relationship Issues. University of Wisconsin-Whitewater, 2000.

[7] Cited in R. L. Van de Castle. *Our Dreaming Mind.* New York: Ballantine Books, 1994, p. 99.

But your thoughts may have focused primarily on a surprise phone call you received from an old friend. Clearly, of all the events, the ones that were most in your thoughts are the ones that most likely will be focused upon in that night's dreams.

Another important point is that when first working with dreams, many people make the mistake of believing the event that connects to your dream is the same as your thoughts -- and so there is no need to record thoughts.

It's important to remember that our thoughts are implicated *in* but actually *separate from* the events. We see this all around us in our everyday lives. Just ask any baseball umpire about calling balls and strikes if you have any doubt about this. Various people interpret the same event in dramatically different ways, based on their own perceptions, biases, needs, fears, and desires.

Even more, our thoughts vary from time to time about same type events. What was once a maddening event (such as locking your keys in your car) can later seem very funny and unimportant. Tragedies, such as the loss of a relationship, may be viewed months or years later as a blessing that helped move you forward in your life.

For this reason, it's important to record your thoughts as accurately as you can remember them and write them in "I thought" statements -- "I thought...." Include when you thought them (yesterday or last evening) so that later, when you return to your dream, you will know you were identifying thoughts instead of suppositions after or before the fact.

A final and very important point about connecting our thoughts with our dreams is this:

When we record our day-before-the-dream thoughts, we are, in fact, writing questions that our dream will be answering.

This sounds a little strange to some people at first, but it's really quite simple and a key to understanding the messages, or "answers," in your dreams.

First, remember that dreams are basically your deeper mind processing images and information and "thinking" about what's very helpful for you -- in short, providing answers for your life. Also, recall that dreams reach to the peripheries of the mind -- further than usual waking thought generally ever goes, which means that we are often only partially aware of these answers, if at all.

This is exactly why many of us sometimes feel stuck or confused in life. We feel as though we need answers, but we do not know how to access the answers from our deeper minds. But, because our dreams come from the deeper regions of the mind, dreams can combine past and current experiences (as Alice's dream has), including intuitive-like wisdom to shed light on our thought-questions.

Although much deeper, the process is similar to what we do consciously in our waking lives when we're trying to make decisions -- say, going to the movies or reading this book, for example. Whichever you decide to do is your "answer" to this problem.

This works the same way with dreams, except that the question or choice you're considering in your dreams isn't always so clear. Just having the answer "read the book" has little meaning unless you're first aware of your choice of either reading or going to the movies.

So, to repeat what we said a bit ago: *When we record our thoughts, we are, in fact, writing questions that our dreams will answer.* In the process of recording our thoughts, and exploring our dreams for connections to these thoughts, we discover the "questions" our dreams address in the context of our waking-life circumstances.

Record the day-or-evening-before-your-dream thoughts after waking from your dream because it is after the dream that connections to specific thought(s) can be made. Record these the same time you record your dream and as they occur to you during the day or evening.

As an alternative, before going to sleep each night record your prominent thoughts (including various thoughts from the day, as well as thoughts about the day's events) in a journal. In this manner, you will have a preview of the "thought-questions" your dream(s) may respond to or answer during the night. This alternative may be beneficial for beginners and for people who have difficulty making connections after the dream.

When we look to our pre-dream thoughts as precursors of our dream, we have a selection of possible questions that impelled our dream. We can relate this to the board game and TV program, *Jeopardy* where the contestant is given the answer, and must supply the question. If we choose to accept our pre-dream incubated words (and not search our pre-dream thoughts), it is akin to accepting only one possible question even before seeing the answer.

So, let's see it in action.

Applying Step 2

Adding to the "events" of PMID Step 1 -- *the book I had been reading that suggested ways to help identify and release anger, and my prayer,* Alice now took a look at her thoughts of the day before her dream. Alice's thoughts that she connected with her dream were:

- *I thought about the tactics the author used in his book that included the inventory exercise. His blatant accusations with cleverly worded ways of keeping those accused from defending themselves because the very defense, in his mind, makes them guilty infuriated me. In my view, the author's accusations were ridiculously and grossly in error. His tactics stirred many memories of my dad's repeated unjust accusations against me when I was a teenager, and I was unable to defend myself because my dad would say my defense proved my guilt. I then decided that I must still be angry with my dad for his accusations during my teenage years.*
- *I also wondered if inventorying my thoughts about my dad could possibly affect him in whatever realm he resides. He died several years ago.*

Some of Alice's other prominent thoughts from the day and evening before this dream were:

- *I thought about the literature lists and wondered if the books I ordered yesterday would arrive in time for me to read before my next physiology class that I am taking.*
- *I thought about the rainbow I saw today and wondered if it could somehow be a confirming sign.*
- *I thought about the differences in people, and specifically the differences between the man who backed out into the traffic lane and the one who came to help.*
- *I thought about my husband's suggestion and wondered if my friend would really benefit from my husband's advice.*

Day-Before-the-Dream Thought Question(s)

To help you further with connecting thoughts to dreams, here are some more examples (associated dreams not included in this writing) of thought questions that brought answering dreams to the dreamers.

- The day before, "I wondered why my feelings toward my spouse had suddenly changed." That night a dream revealed a past circumstance that had shaped the dreamer's current reactions when certain conditions presented themselves.
- "I thought about my mother and how she would not be here for her birthday." That night a dream represented events from the day of the mother's funeral and shed light on the dreamer's over-attention to her mother.
- "I thought about and wondered why I felt the grief so deeply when I learned that my Aunt Joy had died." That night a spiritual teacher came in a dream as a very sad little boy, and had red hair (like Aunt Joy's red hair) though in waking life the spiritual teacher's hair is white. "Aunt Joy's passing affected me deeply because it touched my unconventional, rarely expressed and immature spiritual inclinations. Aunt Joy's openly expressed unconventional ways were often rebuffed by our family group."

When you are searching your memory for clues to your day-before-the dream thoughts that connect to your dream, try mixing concentrated focus with intuitive listening. Also, try recalling thoughts that stirred your emotions during the day. Thoughts fired by emotions are likely candidates to prompt dreams. (At times even sneaky little seemingly unimportant thoughts overshadow major thoughts to prompt a helpful dream.)

Try an experiment to see how thoughts relate to emotions. Purposely think about some event that you consider a "bummer." Notice your associated emotions when you think of the event in terms of it being a discouragement. Now think of some event you consider an "exhilarator." Notice your associated emotions when you think of that event in terms of the event being an encouragement.

Connecting the thoughts described above back to the dream, we see that we can now go another step farther beyond just understanding the overall theme of the dream. **Step 1:** Based on day-before-the-dream

events the dream theme seems to be Alice's *desire to bring to light and address any unresolved feelings of anger toward my dad.*

Step 2: Adding day before the dream **thoughts,** the dream now seems really to focus on *anger toward Dad. A thought question my dream responds to or answers is "Am I still angry with my dad (long after his death) for his unfair accusations of me when I was a teenager?" I want to know if I hold any hidden rage about that and if I do, I want to clear it up.*

As we examine the dream again, we can now see many references to the dreamer, including Alice's thoughts the day before the dream when she was thinking about events of long ago and wondering how she could make it better.

"Old tapes," taking "inventory," "hidden suspicions," an "untended" garden, "old junk" that her dad appears from, and even putting a new coat of paint on her childhood home where these events with her dad took place years ago are all important actions and elements.

By looking at our pre-dream thoughts, we can discover a number of new, obvious, and symbolic connections to the dream. In the process, we've also started into the next PMID step and the one at which most people begin: The symbolism in dreams.

You can now see the importance of the first two PMID steps of identifying (1) Day-before-the-dream events and (2) Day-before-the-dream thoughts. **Both of these steps provide the critical foundation necessary to begin understanding the symbolism in your dream.** Without these steps, you can only guess at the meanings, and you will still have little or no idea how or why these symbols connect with your life.

So, our knowledge of our events and thoughts from before the dream has already given us a clear understanding of what the dream is about and is already making important connections between our dream and our waking life experience.

But what about Alice's dad turning into a tree? Why does her husband show up in her dream at all? Is there something about painting Alice's childhood home (gray vs. some other color) that is a message to her? And we still don't know any more about those other gray buildings that seemed to have popped up for no reason at the end of the dream.

Some of the dream's symbolism is already starting to jump to our attention, and we've already started learning the language of dream symbolism without even trying. So, why stop now, especially since understanding dream symbolism is the purpose of the next PMID Step.

Chapter 4

What's the Connection? PMID STEP 3

In this chapter, we'll discover that the flesh and blood of our dream life, our personal symbolic language, images and memories from the emotional mainstays and epicenters of our lives, are wrapped around our bones. In the PMID Step 3 we will develop our personal definitions of major dream phrases and symbols in the context of this dream, and earlier experiences.

When people ask us, "What does my dream mean?" what they are almost always really asking us is to explain the strange, nonsensical and sometimes frighteningly bizarre things, places and events in their dreams. In short, they are talking about the symbolism in their dreams.

> **PMID Step 3:** Select and define **major dream phrases** and symbols from your write-up of this dream to discover the dream's personalized meanings. Consider effects of day-before-your dream events, thoughts, and earlier experiences on the meaning of each major dream phrase and symbol. The general definition for "phrases" as used in this step is "a string of words." The strings of words can be phrases, clauses, or whole sentences.

Our minds record our experiences and recall them, often symbolic in form, during dreaming. Dreams make connections that are more extensive than is typical during waking thought.[8] Consequently, understanding our personal dream symbolic language has the potential to

---

[8] E. Hartmann. "Making Connections in a Safe Place: Is Dreaming Psychotherapy?" *Dreaming, Journal of the Association for the Study of Dreams* 5(4), 1995, pp. 213-228.

give us insights that we are unaware of in waking states. In short, dreams are our deeper minds working through the same events and thoughts we think about consciously throughout our day, but without the myriad of personal and social restraints as discussed in our Introduction.

That's the good news. The challenge, of course, is making sense of it all. To interpret our dreams for use in the conscious state, we need to understand our own dream symbolism.

The other good news about the symbolism in your dreams is that you've made a great deal of it up all by yourself. Understanding symbolism in your dreams is not about learning and remembering abstract interpretations. It's mostly about understanding your personal dream language that you have created. As Delaney (1996) says, "We are the producers of our own dreams."[9]

Using dream dictionaries

People often use dream dictionaries to help them understand their dream symbols, especially when they first start working with their dreams. Dream dictionaries can be very helpful in providing quick explanations for common dream symbols. These common dream symbols -- also known as *universal* symbols -- are symbols that often have similar meanings for most people.

Dream dictionaries are also helpful as a resource for novice dream interpreters to learn about the breadth of possible symbols. It's not only the talking cows and flying bicycles that are important. More common details, such as whether you're in a house or an office building, which floor or room you're in, and even the color of a building can be important.

But along with positives of using a dream dictionary, we also want to caution against using them.

Dream dictionaries are fine for what they are: a basic reference for universal dream symbols. However, dream dictionaries are *not* explanations of what *your* dream symbolism means for *you*. Synesius of Cyrene (cited in Kelsey, 1991) insisted that the essential nature of dreams

---

[9] G. Delaney. *Living Your Dreams: The Classic Bestseller on Becoming Your Own Dream Expert.* HarperCollins, 1996, p. 5.

is personal. Consequently, only by looking to the dreamer's own experiences can dreams be truly understood.

This is not a minor distinction at all. We understand this obvious difference in our waking lives when we talk with each other. We know that you can't just look up some words to understand the meaning of a sentence. What we say is often not literally what we mean. We all understand that you have to know the context of the conversation, the tone of the speaker, her facial expressions, and whether you're at work or play in order to fully understand what is being said. If you don't know the topic or theme of a conversation, a word or sentence can be pretty hard to make sense of.

These same rules apply with dream symbolism. The more we apply our understanding of our waking life events and thoughts, and explore the general theme and messages of our dreams, the more the individual symbolism will come to life with meaning for us.

So, feel free to use dream dictionaries as thought-starters. Just be sure that you don't confine yourself to the precise definitions described in these.

Dream phrases (and symbols)

It is often very helpful to look for **dream phrases** instead of having to limit yourself to defining the one-word dream symbol by itself. An example of a one-word symbol is door. Universal meanings of the word door are "challenge" and "opportunity." An example of a dream phrase is "locked the car doors," which one dreamer understood to mean, "I think I have to protect myself from danger on the road of life without my spouse." Another dreamer understood "closed the door" to mean he had overcome a difficult relationship issue that was represented in his dream.[10]

Defining whole phrases from the dream helps the dreamer connect definitions to the context of the dream, the context being day-before-the-dream events, day-before-the-dream thoughts, and earlier experiences.

Your ability to bridge the gap from defining one-word symbols to defining dream phrases is very often a major key to capturing the unique-to-you meanings of your dream.

Use of dream phrases comes quite easily to many people. To help get you started we've provided a Dream Phrase Directory in Appendix 1. Use the definitions for dream phrases noted there only as examples, because those are definitions from each dreamer's unique experiences.

When selecting dream phrases to define for your personal definitions, we often find it helpful to select exact phrases, word-for-word from the dream. Your written record of the dream is the closest to your actual dream picture language, so using those exact words often retains the intent of your dream language.

And one final consideration about dream language and symbols in particular: As Freud once said, "Sometimes a cigar is just a cigar." Keep your mind open to symbolic meanings in your dreams, but don't feel that *everything* need have a deep significant purpose. Sometimes we fly in our dreams because of a powerful spiritual awakening in our lives. Other times we fly simply because it's fun and we can. Sometimes a door can represent a new opening or opportunity. And sometimes, it's just a door.

---

[10] E. Duesbury & E. B. Bynum. "Awakening Personal Meanings with Symbol Phrases, Systems Effects, and More," *Dream Network Journal 23*(1), 2004, pp. 34-37.

We strongly recommend that you keep the mantra "less is more" in mind as you begin exploring your dreams in order to avoid confusing yourself by over-interpreting dream symbolism. What's important is to keep your mind open to *what catches your attention most in a dream*. These are always the most significant parts of your dream to understand, and the ones in which the meanings will be most apparent.

Now, let's see all this in action with our example dream. You may want to turn back to the dream for a quick reminder before continuing. (See the dream near the beginning of Section B.) As you read the dream this time, keep your mind open to possible dream phrases and their meanings that you find based on what we've learned from PMID Steps 1 and 2. After you've explored the dream in this new way, continue to see what we've found in the dream.

Applying Step 3

PMID Step 1: Based on **day before the dream events** the dream seems to be Alice's *desire to bring to light and address any unresolved feelings of anger toward my dad.*

PMID Step 2: Adding **day before the dream thoughts** the dream now seems really to focus *on my thought question, "Am I still angry with my dad for unfair accusations of me when I was a teenager?"*

PMID Step 3: Define **dream phrases (and symbols).** Based on our knowledge of the focus and subject of the dream, we can start to make sense of specific phrases in the dream and how they connect to waking life events and thoughts identified in the first two PMID steps. Next are the definitions for the dream phrases and symbols Alice developed for her "Dad and the Inventory Dream."

- ***Tara has left her children in another part of the world:*** *The gap between Tara's true personality (that of a loving concerned mother) and the Tara of the dream. The dream is not about Tara; the dream is picturing me doing something that is not according to my true personality.*

- ***Inventory of all of her furniture:*** *The thought-inventory exercise I was doing. Perhaps furniture represents that I was treating thoughts about my dad as if they were inanimate, lifeless, like furniture instead of alive and full of emotion.*

- ***Old tapes playing her voice saying suspicious things about us:*** *My day-before-the-dream suspicious thoughts that prompted me to do the thought inventory exercise. I was "playing old tapes," going over happenings from the past.*

- ***Sitting on the edge of what seems to be a flowerbed:*** *Ties to last night when I also wondered if inventorying my thoughts about my dad could possibly affect him in whatever realm he resides. Here shows I was on the edge of flowering thoughts about my dad.*

- ***Yard is untended:*** *Not like my family. Shows I neglected my responsibilities and actions while focusing too much only on Dad's activities.*

- ***Seems to be a pile of junk or perhaps junk items beside my husband:*** *Items to throw away, no longer useful.*

- ***Someone covered up with a canvas or tarp—like a sack over his head:*** *Symbolic of "sackcloth and ashes" to me. Sackcloth -- "cloth of mourning and cloth of repentance."*[11] *Probably the sackcloth came in answer to my thoughts about whether my dad suffers because of my remembering and inventorying his transgressions against me. Sackcloth is "a coarse cloth made of goats' hair, which was worn as a sign of mourning or distress."*[12] *Of course, I also suffer when I hold negative thoughts about my dad.*

- ***See that the figure is my dad, who passed away years ago:*** *Refers to old "junk" about Dad that I've been thinking about.*

---

[11] Bible, Authorized King James Version, 1955, p. 229.
[12] Good News Bible, Today's English Version, 1993, p. 1814.

- ***Think that I must be dreaming:*** *Opportunity for me to direct the dream or to deal more consciously with the issues in my dream. The dream is in a lucid state.*

- ***Don't want really to accuse him, it seems—but just to get this rage worked out . . . the rage related to being falsely accused without being allowed to defend myself or he would call my defense proof of my guilt:*** *Shows I don't really want to accuse my dad; the main issue is I want "to get this rage [my rage] worked out" in case I still do hold the rage.*

- ***Dad turns into what appears to be a heavy barked Tree:*** *"Christian symbolism . . . is fully aware of the primary significance of the tree as an axis linking different worlds."*[13]

- ***Plead some with him to stay so we can get this cleared up:*** *While my dad is in the dream, I want to clear up whether I still hold rage I had when I was a teenager of being falsely accused.*

- ***Thomas says something to me—like warning me not to pursue this:*** *My husband, who is himself in this dream, and in a very wise role.*

- ***Tell him [Thomas], "Don't wake me. My dad is here and I want to get this cleared up"—to that effect:*** *My continued insistence of my desire to discover whether I still hold rage for being falsely accused many years ago.*

- ***Standing out at the top of the driveway hill at my parents' farm implement business:*** *The dream changes scenes and takes me back to the actual buildings located on the family property. Here they could signify the building years of my personality, referring to my childhood.*

---

[13] J. E. Cirlot. *A Dictionary of Symbols.* Barnes & Noble, Inc., 1971, p. 347.

- ***Still aware I am dreaming:*** *This is a lucid state in dreaming. In the lucid state, I could have, and did ask a question I wanted to be answered.*

- ***Sun is shining:*** *Good news in this dream.*

- ***"Painting it [the house] gray":*** *Gray color symbolizes I still hold some gray thoughts about my growing up experiences.*

- ***"Area between the top and bottom of the house that isn't painted":*** *Could signify one piece of unfinished business left to deal with in my childhood emotional makeup. The dreaming mind doesn't forget sideline details. A sideline detail in this dream is the unpainted strip on my parents' house, which derives from some years back when I took a major part in painting the family house. We finished it all except one strip.*

- ***All the other buildings are painted gray:*** *Gray color symbolizes I still hold some gray thoughts about my earlier experiences when I lived here.*

- ***Are in fine repair, though:*** *My perceptions about my teenage experiences, are repaired.*

- ***Don't ask why the color is gray or think to ask why the gray color in the dream:*** *Another thought question I could have asked is, Why are all the buildings on my parents' farm implement business gray? Why do I have gray—less than fully colorful, productive thoughts about those experiences having to do with times at my parents' farm implement business gray? Yet, I didn't ask that question during my dream.*

So, how many of these dream phrases and symbols did you discover in the dream? How many others did you see that we didn't address here? Maybe you're wondering why Alice chose some of these and not others. Or maybe you saw slightly differing meanings and are wondering how she can be so sure of these meanings.

Keep in mind that the most important thing in this exercise is the process, not the product. That means this isn't a test to see how many dream phrases and symbols you can correctly identify and can define in

Alice's dream. As we've noted repeatedly, dreams are extremely personal and, therefore, difficult to interpret for someone else. This is an exercise to practice the process of recognizing important dream phrases and symbols and how to connect these with important issues in your life.

We suggest you review these dream phrases and symbols again to see exactly where those listed were in the dream and, further, how these meanings work best for the dreamer, given what you know from PMID Steps 1 and 2. We've also provided exercises later in the book (see Appendix 4) for you to do for additional help.

Suggestions for finding meaning in your own dream phrases and symbols

Most people err to the side of not trying hard enough to find their personal experienced-based meanings to their dream phrases. Try these suggestions to become acquainted with your own personalized dream language.

- First, mentally reason what a particular person, place, object or event could mean to you personally, especially in the context of your day-before-your-dream events and day-before-your dream thoughts that connect to your dream.
- Pose questions to yourself. For example, "What does this building mean? Does it seem familiar in any way?"
- Review your definitions to each of the dream phrases (and symbols), even whole sentences more than once. Review at the time of your first interpretations, and repeat your review during later times, especially for significant dreams. For example, notice the dreamer's response to the phrase **"Don't ask why the color is gray or think to ask why the gray color in the dream"**. The dreamer reports she only noticed that unasked question the third time she reviewed her dream.

- Then shift your thinking to an intuitive feeling mode, and take a break to listen for thoughts to surface in your mind
    - Minute or longer breaks, long walks, for example, can be helpful in clearing your mind if you're feeling stuck about a dream phrase or symbol.
    - Listen to the quick or intuitive "thought" (it is a surety, even a body feel, that the quick thought is correct).
        - "That building feels like the house in which I grew up. Aha!"

To summarize, defining dream phrases and symbols are the most important keys to finding meanings in your dreams. Yet, understanding your dreaming language can be like learning a new spoken language, even though it is your personal dreaming language. So, be diligent and patient as you work with understanding what the dream phrases and symbols in your dreams represent to you. You will find once you become acquainted with your dream code, dream phrases and symbol meanings will be "neither mysterious nor inaccessible."[14]

Selecting key dream phrases is a judgment evaluation by the dreamer as to which dream phrases are the most personally meaningful. A dreamer's spontaneous feelings are the best gauges for knowing the relative accuracy of meanings she or he has developed. Selecting dream phrases from the exact words you recorded in your dream narrative will help you catch the unique-to-you meaning of your dream language.

Dreamers frequently notice that some of their dream symbols repeat themselves. Repeated dream symbols can vary in meaning from dream to dream depending on the context of the dream. The thing to keep in mind is the need to be flexible in defining your dream phrases and symbols.

The PMID model was developed both to help open your mind to the symbolic language of dreams and meanings and to provide additional ways to "check" yourself, wherein you'll find that some dream phrases and symbols will come to life with more richness and others may not seem

---

[14] R. Cartwright & L. Lamberg. *Crisis Dreaming, Using Your Dreams to Solve Your Problems.* ASJA *Press,* 2000, p. 5.

as important as you work with the dream. In fact, the rest of the PMID steps are designed to help you learn even more about your dreams, dream phrases, and symbols.

Chapter 5

What Did You feel? PMID STEP 4

Imagine what life would be like without emotions; without the color, the vibrancy, the dense richness of feeling emotions bring. At more difficult times in our lives it may seem that life would be at least a little easier. But, we'd also miss out on all the beauty and joys to which we are all drawn as well. The events of our lives, our thoughts, experiences, achievements and even deepest relationships, would become nothing more than a series of sterile punctuations in reality. Without emotions, human life would lose perhaps all it's meaning.

Once again, our dreams work in a similar fashion to our waking life. So far, we have examined the events and thoughts in our dreams and discovered the myriad of ways they can be represented in our dreams through symbolism. Each provides important groundwork to understanding what our dream is about. But now it's time to get to the heart of the matter -- literally and figuratively -- by exploring the emotions and literal life of our dreams.

> **PMID Step 4:** Compare your **dreaming emotions** with your **waking life emotions** about the main issue and/or relationship in this dream. What differences, if any, do you find between your dreaming emotions and waking life emotions? Also, periodically review your dreaming emotions about the main issue or relationship.

What we do not understand we often tend to fear. What we do understand tends to give us hope and courage. In this chapter, we will make a further connection between what we feel during the rational restrained confines of the day and our wider roaming travels of the night.

In PMID Step 4, we will help you compare your dreaming emotions with your waking life emotions. What differences, if any, will you find between your dreaming and waking life emotions about the primary issues and relationships in your dreams? Also, periodically, you will be able to study and compare your dreaming emotions over time about these core issues and relationships that are the backdrop of your life.

Synesius (about 365-414 AD) understood that people can benefit by making these comparisons. He said dreams reveal joy and fear. As a consequence, the dream makes it possible to "prolong our pleasure by seizing joy" and "guard against and repel [fear]" . ... "These hopes have such force that he [sic] who is bound in fetters, whenever he permits the will of his to hope, is straightway unbound" (p. 10).

Emotions powered by thoughts are fundamental features of waking life. Emotions powered by waking thoughts are also fundamental features of dreams. A major difference is that dreams guided by emotions paint things on a more fluid canvas and "make connections more widely, more broadly than waking thoughts."[15]

For this reason, exploring dreaming emotions is a valuable technique for understanding our deepest waking-life emotions. Once again, our dreaming lives are not as self-censored by what is right or the various "shoulds" that permeate our everyday lives. We are free to -- in fact, cannot help but -- more fully experience and express our full range of emotions about issues in our lives.

Not only do we more fully experience our current emotions in our dreams, our minds also draw from similar experiences and emotions from our past for clarification and answers regarding how to deal with our current issues. For example,

> Suppose a recent event results in tension, which continues to trouble the dreamer. The feelings connected with this issue surface during REM sleep and are represented in the initial images of a dream. . . . Faced with whether or not it is safe to remain asleep, the dreamer has to check out the intruding stimulus by exploring how the past can

---

[15] E. Hartmann. *Dreams and Nightmares, The Origin and Meaning of Dreams.* Perseus Publishing, 1998, p. 11.

shed light on it. The feelings connected with this issue surface (during sleep). . . The dreamer pulls upon his or her memory bank, which is programmed with the initial images of the dream and the feelings associated with them. A flock of images from the past swiftly emerge. These images sometimes go all the way back to childhood, and are in some way related to the current issue.[16]

This example again illustrates how and why emotions play such an important role in your dreams. Plus, it reminds us that the symbolism in dreams is self-created, meaning that they are *your* personal symbols created by *your* mind based on the context of *your* life.

Fully experiencing our emotions can certainly be a very freeing experience. How wonderful it is to feel, say and do whatever our hearts desire. But, this can also be rather troubling. The experience can sometime be very difficult and stressful. This is particularly true of our most painful or threatening emotions.

As adults, we are extremely well-practiced at withholding or tempering our emotions. As we've addressed previously, society could not exist if we weren't. Social conformity, rules, and just plain common courtesy are all important to maintaining social order and, in turn, our comfort and security in the world.

However, we have also become just as skilled at denying our emotions to ourselves. The same social constructs that are essential to helping us all live more harmoniously as a group lead us to internalize these rules to our personal detriment. We try to "control" our emotions internally, as well as externally.

In some cases, this has the obvious benefit of helping to calm or soothe ourselves and minimize the risk of our emotions running away with us. In short, it prevents us from "losing it," such as a child does when he throws a tantrum.

The downside is that we can easily lose touch with what we really feel as individuals. We become so good at managing and controlling our

---

[16]S. Krippner & J. Dillard. *Dreamworking, How to Use Your Dreams for Creative Problem-Solving*. Buffalo, NY: Bearly Limited, 1988, p. 52.

emotions, we're able to shut off our awareness of "bad" emotions before we're even fully aware of what we're feeling.

The result is that we can often find ourselves feeling confused about what we really do feel or want in life. We struggle to find our emotional footing and, failing that, often feel lost, adrift, or just generally stuck with little sense of direction or purpose.

In addition to gaining a deeper and more meaningful understanding of our emotions and ourselves, our intent in PMID Step 4 is also to reduce stress levels. It's one thing to recognize negative emotions but quite another to know what you can do to reduce these stressful emotions. Dreams are keys to discovering how exactly to do this.

As you read on and begin to apply this PMID Step 4 to your own dream work, we encourage you to be very diligent and honest in identifying dreaming emotions accurately. These are your dreams, so it's important to be aware of any feelings and move beyond any worry that your dreaming emotions are "telling on you." Worry over dream revelations is simply a waking life reaction that is misplaced in working with your dreams. What is important is to let yourself see and experience your emotions openly, honestly, and non-judgmentally and to discover the answers they hold for you.

If your dreams are especially troubling, you may want to consider talking with a counseling professional. While such need could be infrequent, having a trusted resource and support person can greatly reduce levels of stress and help you learn and grow from your dream experiences in positives ways. For more information about what to look for in your dreams if you are having emotional trouble and need to see someone professionally, please read "A Caveat on Bad or Worrisome Dreams" in our "Considerations for Dreamwork in Clinical Settings" at the end of this Section B.

Exploring your dreaming emotions

In the first two steps, we asked you to record events and thoughts from your *waking life* to provide a theme and context to understand what your dream was about. In Step 3, we began looking at the dream itself to uncover and understand the symbolic language of the dream, based on your waking life events and thoughts.

Now, in Step 4 we will continue to explore the dream with a focus on your *dreaming* emotions. Record your dreaming emotions within the dream itself to remind you that dreaming emotions are essential parts of the dream and in order to retain a record of your dreaming emotions. As in Steps 1 and 2, it's important to write this down as soon as you can after you awaken from the dream because this is when the emotions will be the freshest.

After you have noted your emotions from the dream, compare your dreaming emotions with your before-your-dream waking life emotions. What differences, if any, do you find between your dreaming emotions and waking life emotions about the main issue and or relationship in this dream? Also, compare your dreaming emotions over time about the main issue or relationship. What seems to be changing? What emotions are reoccurring, suggesting that you may be stuck on an issue?

This step of noticing changes in emotions over time is a valuable tool in traditional counseling as well. Carl Jung compared dreams to a barometer[17] because for him emotions measure the one-sidedness of our attitudes. Psychiatrist-researcher Milton Kramer[18] described dreams as emotional thermostats. Prominent dream investigators have found that dreams (though often exaggerated) are intrinsically honest sources of information about our factory of emotions.[19] The intrinsic honesty of emotional content in dreams helps you, the dreamer, set your dreams

---

[17] C. G. Jung. *Two Essays on Analytical Psychology*. R. F. C. Hull, Trans., Princeton, NJ: Bollingen Series/Princeton University Press, 1966.

[18] M. Kramer, "The Selective Mood Regulatory Function of Dreaming: An Update and Revision," In A. Moffitt, M. Kramer and R. Hoffman (Eds.) *The Functions of Dreaming*. NY: State University of New York Press, 1993, pp.139-195.

[19] C. G. Jung. *Two Essays on Analytical Psychology* (R. F. C. Hull, Trans., Princeton, NJ: Bollingen Series/Princeton University Press, 1966; L. Caligor & R. May. *Dreams and Symbols: Man's Unconscious Language*. NY: Basic Books, 1968; A. Faraday. *The Dream Game*. NY: Harper & Row, 1974; B. B. Wolman & M. Ullman. *Handbook of States of Consciousness*. NY: Van Nostrand Reinhold Company, 1986.

within your recent emotional experiences, and, consequently, helps you apply your dreams to your life.[20]

As you explore your dreaming emotions and compare them to your before-dream cognitive identification of your emotions about a relationship or issue, search for symbolic representations of dream emotions as well as objective representations. For examples, poisoning another person in a dream could represent passing negative tendencies on to another person; a pat on the back could mean just that -- commendation.

Stressful emotions often derive from relationship issues.[21] When dreams center on relationship issues, likelihood for dreamwork to help the dreamer understand and reduce stressful relationship issues, as well as understand and enhance healthy relationships, seems great.

As you begin to work with this step, at times you may say, "Okay, my dreaming emotions show that I have stressful relationships with another person. Guess what? I already know I don't like that person. I already think about it all the time. So, how does the dream give me any additional insights or help me figure out how to deal with the situation?"

The next PMID step deals with this directly. But for now just keep in mind that dreams often contain suggestions for changing thoughts, attitudes or behavior in order to relieve stress. Other times dreams confirm what we already know and then add bits of wisdom beyond what we are cognizant of. For example, "The wisdom of dreams can guide us to successfully resolve the challenges of life transitions by allowing us to identify and reclaim powerful hidden feelings that undermine our ability to move forward."[22]

---

[20] C. G. Jung. *Two Essays on Analytical Psychology* (R. F. C. Hull, Trans., Princeton, NJ: Bollingen Series/Princeton University Press, 1966.

[21] C. S. Hall. The Meaning of Dreams. Harper & Row, 1966; Ullman & Zimmerman. *Working With Dreams*. NY: Delacorte Press/Alice Friede, 1979; B. B. Wolman & M. Ullman. *Handbook of States of Consciousness*. NY: Van Nostrand Reinhold Company, 1986.

[22] A. Siegel. *Dream Wisdom, Uncovering Life's Answers in Your Dreams*. (Celestial Arts), 2002, p. 18.

If you are having reoccurring dreams about a stressful situation in your waking life, it is often a signal that this is something you should be addressing more directly than you likely are.

If some of your dreaming emotions seem obvious, look closer at these by examining the specific events or context in which you're having these emotions in your dreams.

For example, if you encounter an irritating co-worker in your dream and feel angry, try to notice the details of this encounter, such as the location and what each of you are doing. If you're talking on the phone in your dream when the person appears, it may suggest that you should communicate with her directly; or the phone could be a strong emphasis to listen to the message in the dream. On the other hand, if you're dreaming that you're talking with a policeman and this other person appears, it may suggest that you should discuss the issue with someone in authority; or it could be a caution about your interactions with this person. Similarly, dreaming that this person is in your house could suggest that you need to establish stronger personal boundaries to prevent this person's invasion of your personal emotional space; or it could be the person symbolizes some aspect of your current mindset. Or, if the house is a former house, it could indicate that how you are currently reacting to this person is how you reacted at another time in your life to someone else. In all cases it is important to consider the context of the dream.

We will discuss more about the dream's problem-solving suggestions in the next chapter when Alice finds answers to her pre-dream thought-questions. Now let's take a look at our dreaming emotions and compare them to our waking life emotions.

Applying Step 4 - Compare your **dreaming emotions** with your **waking life emotions** about the main issue of the dream.

Alice, the dreamer, wrote for this step, *In my dream, I feel surprise that Tara leaves her children, and I am shocked that Tara is suspicious of my husband and me. In contrast, in my waking life before this dream I did not consider whether the inventorying exercise would divert me from more important personality matters, so I was unaware of any surprise or shock emotions about what I was doing.*

In waking life, I was intensely upset from reading the book and then connecting being upset to my dad. At first, I did not understand why the author's words would bother me so much, and I was surprised how greatly the book affected me. Then I realized some of the author's techniques and judgments reminded me of some of my dad's reprimands of me when I was younger. If I became angry about my dad's criticisms, he would say that my anger proved my guilt. I would go to my room and quote: "And, ye fathers, provoke not your children to wrath."[23]

My dreaming emotions are also illustrated by the color gray. All the buildings are painted gray. Yet, in waking life all these buildings are white. To me the color gray reveals my waking life downcast emotions about the past. Yet during my dream I didn't even question why all the buildings on my parents' farm implement business were gray.

I also recorded dreaming emotions about being glad that my dad came in the dream so I could get my anger with him worked out. My waking life emotions about the prospect of exploring and getting any anger worked out were anxious hopefulness.

As the above dream plainly shows, Alice's dreaming mind reached beyond her current inventorying thoughts about her dad; her dream reached back to the family home and business to show that her current suspicious emotions had clouded what had been white and sunny -- positive in her emotions about her dad.

The surprise we discovered as we've gone deeper into her dream is that her suspicions and concerns that originated from her cognitive thought inventorying exercise weren't true at all. The dream clearly showed these were just "old tapes" that were no longer relevant to her life and didn't need to be dealt with.

As you can see, waking life thoughts and impressions can sometimes be off base. Identifying our dream emotions is one of the best ways to check ourselves to make sure that we are interpreting our waking life thoughts and impressions correctly.

Interestingly, recording emotions within the dream is historically the most neglected part of dream recording. Can you imagine talking with a friend or counselor about an event in your life and not even mentioning

---

[23] Bible, King James Version, *Ephesians, 6:4*. The World Publishing Company, Cleveland and New York.

how you felt about it? Clearly, our feelings are just as important in understanding our dreams as they are in our waking life.

In this current chapter, we've gone beyond events, thoughts and symbolism to confirm how we felt about these events. In short, we know all about the dream, but there's still something missing— the answer to the question: "Now that I know what my dream is telling me, what should I do in my waking life to fix it?"

> *"Who of us has not had a dream of a lover or a relative or a friend that expressed precisely the nature, the depth, and the tone of our relationship to them?"*
>
> -- Edward Bruce Bynum, *Families and the Interpretation of Dreams*

Chapter 6

What Should You Do? PMID STEP 5

"A dream that is not interpreted and understood is like a letter that we fail to open."

Attributed to various writers -- one is Rabbi Hisda, Israel leader in the early years of Christianity

In the PMID Step 5 we are going to explore the dream. We are going to open the letter given to us by the night visitors for possible suggestions as to how to change our thoughts, attitudes and behavior that will, in turn, lead us to a clearer understanding of ourselves and a reduction in the stress that sometimes surrounds key issues.

> **PMID Step 5:** Explore your dream for possible **solutions** to problems or **suggestions** for changing (or affirming) your thoughts, attitudes, or behaviors. Consider your responses to each PMID model step, including Step 6, as you search for solutions and suggestions in this dream. Give primary attention to the power of your before-your-dream thoughts (PMID step 2) to act as questions that your dream answers.

The simplest application of Step 5 is first to review the day-before-your dream thought(s) (Step 2) that you connect to your dream. Treat the thought(s) as a question(s) that your dream answers. Then explore your responses to all the other PMID steps (including Step 6) for solutions or suggestions. (Note: We placed Step 6 after Step 5 because only the first five steps are necessary for other than relationship type dreams.)

A major outcome assessment in family counseling is problem solving.[24] A major outcome of use of the PMID model is the dreamer's ability to discover problem-solving suggestions as noted in the following:

> This method [PMID model] is especially helpful in identifying, clarifying, and resolving relationship problems. During our waking hours, we often feel frustrated that our rational attempts to solve life challenges are unsuccessful. It is then that our dreams often provide innovative and unexpected answers.[25]

Obviously, we all have consciously developed insights into how to change unproductive and upsetting thoughts, attitudes and behaviors. But, we've also all faced the frustrations of not really knowing what to do, and sometimes being confused about what the problem really is that we're trying to solve. Should we leave a bad relationship or work situation, or is there some way to fix it? Is there something that we may be unintentionally doing or feeling that we can change to make things better? How do we stop that frustrating and familiar cycle of taking steps to resolve a situation only to see it end up the same or sometimes worse?

A dream bringing insights about the association between earlier experiences and current reactions can be the answer. As we've discussed, dreamwork will bring new insights about waking events, thoughts, and emotions. Consequently, after a day of emotional experiences, intense or not-so-intense experiences, that night you may have a dream that suggests solutions to alleviate emotional stress associated with your daytime experiences.

---

[24] S. Benish . "Assessing Family Interventions," In *Family Counseling for all Counselors*. Greensboro, North Carolina: Co-publishers -- Eric Clearing house on Counseling and Student Services, American Counseling Association Foundation, 2003, pp. 161-174.
[25] S. Krippner. Co-author of *Dreamworking, How to Use Your Dreams for Creative Problem Solving*.

"By using your dreams for creative problem-solving you may also be able to increase your options and encounter new ways of thinking, feeling, and behaving that will enrich your life and actualize your potentials."[26]

People have reported problem-solving dreams since earliest recorded history. "Many of the things which present difficulties to us awake, some of these it makes completely clear while we are asleep, and others it helps us explain."[27] The dream provides answers to the thought-questions put to it.[28] As a result, we can examine our dreams for answers to important thought-questions.

Dreams also reflect successful behavior modifications. From there, we can interject Perls'[29] concept that life is "an infinite number of unfinished situations -- incomplete gestalts."[30] When one issue melts into the background, another gestalt, or issue, moves to the foreground to be addressed.

Dreams work in very much the same way as modern therapy approaches. For example, in existential therapy people gain awareness and self-consciousness of their relationship to their self. Self-consciousness leads to insight. Insight is curative because now the individual sees the possibility of doing something about problems.[31]

Also in Gestalt therapy, self-awareness of sensation and expression by itself is curative.[32] The self-enhancement gained from interpreting dreams can lead to change in the dreamer.[33] Repeated dream

---

[26] S. Krippner & J. Dillard. *Dreamworking, How to Use Your Dreams for Creative Problem-Solving.* Buffalo, NY: Bearly Limited, 1988, p. 248.

[27] Synesius of Cyrene. cited in Kelsey 1991, p. 248, par. 9

[28] G. Delaney. "The Dream Interview," In G. Delaney (Ed.), *New Directions in Dream Interpretation.* Albany, NY: State University of New York Press, 1993, pp. 195-240.

[29] F. Perls. *Gestalt Therapy Verbatim.* Lafayette, CA: Real People Press, 1969.

[30] F. Perls. *Gestalt Therapy Verbatim.* Lafayette, CA: Real People Press, 1969, p. 15.

[31] R. May, *The Discovery Of Being.* NY: W. W. Norton & Company, 1983.

[32] E. Polster & M. Polster. *Gestalt Therapy Integrated.* NY: Brunner/Mazel Publishers, 1973.

[33] M. Kramer. "The Selective Mood Regulatory Function of Dreaming: An Update and Revision," In A. Moffitt, M. Kramer and R. Hoffman (Eds.). *The Functions of Dreaming.* NY: State University of New York Press, 1993, pp.139-195.

interpretations over time leads to insight, and insight leads to behavioral change.[34]

Keep in mind the proviso that only you, the dreamer, have the potential to know ultimately with certainty whether the suggestions you find are accurate. Also, keep in mind that the suggestions and solutions your dream brings are most often for you -- not for another.

So, in Step 5 we continue to build on all the previous PMID Steps to discover suggestions your dreams hold for specific actions you can take to resolve your problems in waking life. So far we've been able to translate the highly symbolic language of the dream into a solid understanding of what part of our waking life the dream is really about by connecting our pre-dream events and thoughts in PMID Steps 1 and 2, interpreting the dream symbolism in Step 3, and also understanding our deeper dreaming emotions in Step 4. We are now ready to search our dream for solutions.

Applying PMID Step 5 - Explore your dream for possible **solutions or suggestions** on changing thoughts, attitudes or behaviors (answer[s] to day-before-my-dream thoughts).

Alice, the dreamer wrote for this step, *I had believed that because of the anger I was feeling -- caused by the emotional inventory exercise -- that I had not really gotten over these emotions and needed to continue to work on getting over them. My dream replies to my yesterday's thought plus answers my prayer, and it says the opposite, that I no longer feel rage toward my dad for falsely accusing me, and there is no need to keep dwelling on this.*

It is obvious to me that my dream suggests to stop the inventorying exercise. Nothing is positive about the inventory symbolism in the dream.

Also, I need to stop accusing my dad, whether it is about the false accusations or about the unpainted strip on the house -- whatever the unpainted strip represents.

---

[34] S. B. Spiegel & C. A. Hill. "Guidelines for Research on Therapist Interpretation: Toward Greater Methodological Rigor and Relevance to Practice," *Journal of Counseling Psychology* 36(1), 1989, pp. 121-129.

Dad's weary look shows that though, as I say in the dream, "I don't want really to accuse him," the inventorying process is accusing him. I know that blaming another only avoids my responsibility for changing my unhelpful thoughts and emotions that result in stress to me.

Finally, my dream shows I needed to have thought to ask in the dream why the gray color for all the buildings on the family business.

Alice recognizes that blaming another, even the person involved in the earlier experience, here, her dad, will only intensify her stress. With the PMID model the idea is for the dreamer to take responsibility for changing thoughts, attitudes and behavior to alleviate the stress she or he feels.

Clearly, Alice's dream is telling her that she doesn't need to worry about her anger toward her dad for unjust criticisms anymore. While these old emotions can still be stirred (through the inventory exercise in this case), it is not benefiting her growth to revisit them, as they are not issues in her current life. She was needlessly bringing up past pain about her dad and, in the process, causing her unnecessary stress.

Alice also found suggestions for future work. *"Recognize that my negative attitudes about Dad came up from my inventorying exercise, and not from an issue I need to address."* In the future, she doesn't need to revisit this question of anger at her dad about unjust criticisms. Alice also found *"the dream suggests there may be some other unfinished business that I should be open to understanding, signified by the unpainted strip on my old house."*

Is *that* something from the past still lingering? Since it's just one little unpainted strip, it's likely not extremely significant, yet it will be helpful for her to keep her mind open to clues for even greater discoveries about herself.

A thought question Alice could have asked within her dream is, *Why are all the buildings on my parents' farm implement business gray?* Why Do I have lingering—less than fully colorful productive thoughts—about my experiences at the family farm implement business?

Is *that* something from the past still lingering? Obviously, it would be helpful for Alice to explore any of her dreams that may contain suggestions on the origin of those gray thoughts, whether they still linger in her mind, and, if so, how to overcome those negative perceptions.

As a brief commentary, sensitivity to reactions from earlier experiences is a very significant discovery to which many people can easily relate. We've all experienced pain and hurt in our lives -- events in which we can all easily go back to and quickly stir up in order to relive those sometimes very intense negative emotions. But does just being able to re-experience the pain mean that the issue is unresolved? More importantly, how do you know?

If you're unsure, you may end up unnecessarily revisiting past hurt, wasting emotions on people and events, and needlessly re-opening old wounds, long since healed, by hanging onto the past. On the flip side, simply ignoring painful past events may result in continually burying important emotions only to see them surface again and again throughout your life and resulting in that common feeling of being "stuck."

In this case, Alice's dream has shown her that just because she felt strong negative emotions about the past, it is not an indication these feelings are unresolved or that she needs to dwell on these. In fact, the dream helped her realize that she really was over this anger toward her dad (the "old junk") and that the best thing for her to do was to move on.

In summary, Alice is now clear about what exactly her concerns were, and in this step she has recognized a workable, beneficial solution to her pre-dream thought questions.

The unpainted strip and the gray buildings still remain a mystery at this point, but they are also wonderful hints to future self-discovery. Our dreams often reference other dreams we've had. In this case, keeping the unpainted strip of this dream and the gray buildings in mind could help her connect to answers presented in future dreams. We'll also discuss in Section C how to work with a series of dreams and recognize these references between dreams.

At this point, it may be there is nothing more we can learn from the dream. We understand the waking life problem, the dream's message, and its suggestion for Alice's waking life. What else could be there?

What's left is the piece that is the basis for many psychological approaches in use today, yet is almost completely ignored in many other dream interpretation models.

If you currently happen to live on a desolate island with no human contact at all, and have no memories of your family or any relationships from your past, then this last step of the PMID process might not be obvious to you.

However, if you have any relationships in your life of any kind, be they with family members, friends, parents, a spouse, children, or co-workers, then you'll immediately understand the critical importance of this next step.

As we've said many times, our dreams reflect our waking lives. But if that's true, what was Alice's husband doing in the dream? Her emotions about her dad were based on events that happened *many* years before she ever met her husband; so, what's her husband doing in this dream? And why were her brothers or sisters -- those who actually experienced these events with Alice -- completely missing from her dream?

Chapter 7

Who's In Your Dream?
PMID STEP 6

For PMID Step 6 you will explore and comment on your relationship with and reactions to each major person represented in your dream. What did you "do" in the dream and what do you do in waking life in reaction to the people and circumstances portrayed in this dream?

PMID Step 4 is for comparing dreaming and waking life emotions: PMID Step 6 is for comparing dreaming and waking life *reactions* to each person in the dream. We will also see explicitly how the dream reflects the effects of your earlier experiences in similar circumstances.

"The wisdom of dreams can guide us . . . by alerting us to wounds from the past that have reemerged to plague us in the present."[35] When we make healthy changes in our reactions to others, circumstances on all levels change.

> **PMID Step 6:** Explore your dream for **family and other relationship systems perspectives** (influences arising from reactions to family and other major relationships, past and current) to discover whether this dream reflects your reactions during earlier experiences with your family or other major relationships. Compare and comment on your dreaming and your waking life reactions to the primary relationships in this dream. (If this dream is not about a relationship, type the words "Not Applicable" in this space.)

---

[35] A. Siegel. *Dream Wisdom, Uncovering Life's Answers in Your Dreams.* Celestial Arts, 2002, p. 18.

We all react to others in some way, and these reactions are the causes of many feelings and often behaviors.

An age-old example is the story of the guy whose boss yelled at him, so he arrives home from work in a bad mood and kicks the family dog. Played out further, his kicking the family dog could, in turn, cause his child to react by bursting into tears, to which his wife may become angry and accuse him of being a bad father. Her reaction could easily be driven by her own childhood experiences of her father always coming home angry from work and making her cry, or possibly by her disappointment in wanting to enjoy a nice evening with her family that is now seemingly ruined. A whole chain reaction of emotions was triggered by one interaction between the man and his boss. Yet, our guy may not understand his boss' anger was triggered not by him at all, but by the boss' recent argument with a friend.

This is the *systems effect* and our lives are filled with personal experiences of it.

The above story is obviously a negative example of the systems effect. However, the opposite is just as true.

If one person can improve his or her reactions to other people in a group of relationships, the group of relationships must adjust to accommodate that one person's change.[36]

The dreamwork systems approach is a new dreamwork concept. With a dreamwork systems approach, instead of having the family or group together as would typically happen in a counseling session, the individual gathers and studies (either alone or with a counselor) dreams about major relationships in his or her life, primarily related to the family.

Reactions to others based on earlier experiences -- the *systems effect* -- can be very difficult to recognize in our waking lives, especially since most of us have established our patterns over years, often since early childhood. The good news is that once you begin to recognize negative patterns, you can immediately begin to change the dynamic.

---

[36] D. M. Allen. *A Family Systems Approach to Individual Psychotherapy.* Northvale, New Jersey: Jason Aronson, Inc., 1994.

One person's reactions do affect how others react. That means you don't have to change everyone around you (nor can you). But you can change your own thoughts, emotions and actions, and these will absolutely change your relationships with others.

Initially, many people hesitate at making changes in themselves to address relationship issues. This is especially true if the other person seems obviously to be the cause of the problem. The common reaction is, "Why should I change when I haven't done anything wrong, and the other person is creating all the problems?"

It's not unusual to feel that you're letting the other person off the hook, or that you are somehow admitting to being the "bad" person because you're taking responsibility for your role in the relationship.

Certainly, "others" have issues to work through. But the PMID dream interpretation model is based on decades of psychological practice that repeatedly demonstrates it is not a matter of who is at fault -- it's a matter of changing who we can change most successfully . . . our own selves.

Dreams also reflect repeated emotional patterns within relationship systems from generation to generation, [37] again reflecting what is happening in our waking lives. "In the case of a healthy family system, [explorations into dreams] can increase true empathy and acceptance of differences, thus avoiding irresolvable conflicts." [38] In the case of conflicting relationships, an individual's explorations into dreams can yield suggestions for changing thoughts, attitudes and behavior currently, and reduce the possibility of conflicting patterns getting repeated in the next generation.

Now back to Alice, her dream, and how all of this comes into play in the final step of fully understanding her dream.

Applying PMID Step 6

---

[37] E. B. Bynum. *Families and the Interpretation of Dreams: Awakening the Intimate Web.* Paraview Books, 2003.
[38] E. B. Bynum. *The Family Unconscious.* Wheaton, IL: The Theosophical Publishing House, 1984, p. 31.

PMID Step 1: Based on **day-before-the-dream events,** the dream seems to be Alice's *desire to bring to light and address any unresolved feelings of anger toward my dad.*

PMID Step 2: Adding **day-before-the-dream thoughts,** the dream now seems really to focus *on my thought question, "Am I still angry with my dad for unfair accusations of me when I was a teenager?"*

PMID Step 3: Define **dream phrases and symbols.** Based on the first two PMID steps, Alice, the dreamer, identified a series of important dream phrases and symbols: *Tara coming back alone without her children; inventory of furniture; old tapes playing suspicious things about us; our untended yard; realize I am dreaming; Dad coming out of the junk pile; long tarpaulin/canvas-like sack; Dad turning into a tree; repaired buildings on the family property; unpainted strip on the house.*

PMID Step 4: Compare your **dreaming emotions** with your **waking life emotions.** Now during comparisons of dreaming and waking life emotions our dreamer, Alice, *discovered my dreaming emotions were a shock about what I was doing with the inventory exercise, something I had not considered in waking life. I also discovered a difference in my dreaming emotions about my dad and my waking suspicions about repressed anger at him.*

PMID Step 5: Solution(s) found for changing thoughts, attitudes or behaviors (answer[s] to day-before-my-dream **thoughts**). Based on her PMID interpretations so far, Alice found dream-suggested solutions to her day-before-the-dream thought questions: *I am no longer angry with my dad for his unfair accusations of me when I was a teenager. Also, stop the inventorying exercise. Stop blaming my dad about whatever happened in experiences with him. Blaming him causes otherwise up-looking sunny emotions to turn negative and gray. And, search for what the unpainted strip on the house and the gray buildings signify. Are those some things from the past still bothering me?*

PMID Step 6 -- Dreaming and waking life **reactions** to each person in this dream.

Alice's response to Step 6 is, *My dad is the primary relationship in this dream. As my interpretations of this dream clearly show, I reacted strongly to his criticisms. My kinder reactions to Dad in the dream when we were back at the family property are similar to my reactions to Dad when not in the heat of a disagreement. His kindness at those times had and continues to have healthy effects for me.*

Other systems effects I see from working with this dream are that my youthful reactions to Dad's criticisms intensified my current reaction to the inventory book's author, who used similar judgmental tactics as Dad. I can be aware currently of my sensitivity to help myself when I am (or think I am) being falsely accused, so I can avoid letting my emotions overwhelm me.

Further, I can also be aware of the effect my sensitivity to criticism -- constructive, as well as not constructive -- may have on my interactions with my family and other major relationships. This discovery also leads me to wonder if my sensitivity has affected them in ways that I have been unaware of before now, and if so how?!

Other systems effects are suggested by the buildings in my dream that are already painted gray. Am I retaining negative reactions from my earlier experiences in any of my current reactions to others?

My husband Thomas is also a significant character in my dream, and his presence reaffirms both my feelings of trust in his wisdom (when Thomas is suggesting to me that I do not need to pursue old issues with my dad, just as the later parts of the dream convey) and his love and caring for my well-being (his steady presence by the pile of "old junk"). While reaffirming my positive feelings for my husband, it also leads me to ask myself if I sometimes dismiss his advice too quickly, especially when I'm upset (as I did in the dream when I wanted to work things out with my dad rather than listen to Thomas' advice to let it go).

Reflections on Alice's exploration of systemic effects

An important point to note in Alice's interpretation is that she not only recognizes her relationship dynamics with the main characters in her dream, but she also goes a step farther to ask herself in what other relationships in her waking life might these dynamics be playing out.

In this final step, we see how Alice is able to go a step farther to see more clearly her own perceptions of others, the ways she may be misinterpreting others' intentions and the specific steps she can take to make changes in herself to help prevent or at least minimize future negative interactions with other people in her life.

This is an excellent example of the *systems effect* we've discussed at length, and the reason why PMID Step 6 is so important and can have such a profoundly positive effect on your life. In this step, we are able to go far beyond the primary messages of the specific dream and apply our deeper understanding of key relationships so as to build a variety of different relationships throughout our lives. In short, even if you don't have a specific dream about a problematic relationship (such as with a close friend), you can help lessen the pain and frustration of the relationship simply by applying what you learn about yourself in your dreams!

While Step 6 is the last in the PMID process, this whole process is really just the first step in creating an ongoing relationship with yourself.

Many, if not most people start their exploration in dreamwork because of one or maybe two very significant (and often times reoccurring) dreams. If your goal is to understand a particular dream, the PMID process can be extraordinarily helpful in solving its mysteries. As we've seen, the PMID process doesn't require years of training or dreamwork practice, and it works extremely well for interpreting a single dream.

Some people decide to stop there, and there's certainly nothing wrong with that. At the same time, we can also tell you that when people discover a deeper understanding of a significant dream it most often leads to a greater curiosity about what other secrets their dreams may hold; this is where dreamwork really becomes exciting.

In some ways, interpreting a dream for the first time is not unlike your first meeting with a new friend. You can immediately discover a number of fascinating and interesting things about your new friend, but you also quickly learn that there's much more to learn about the person.

And once again, our dreams reflect our lives. They grow and develop as our understanding and appreciation of them grows, just as any relationship that we spend more and more time with does. Whereas we have fully explored this single dream from Alice, it also gives us clues as to what more her dreams may hold for her in the future.

Remember that unpainted strip on her old family house, and the gray buildings? Alice never did figure out what those mean did she -- except they must have something to do with unfinished business, unresolved issues. They could have been nothing. They may be a connection that will come to her much later in life. What we know for sure is that if there are significant unresolved concerns, the symbolism in some form will reappear in her dreams again when she strings more dreams together.

This concept of learning to string together the meanings of multiple dreams is often referred to as a *dream series*, and learning to understand the correlations of multiple dreams during the course of time can increase understanding of yourself exponentially. Obviously, the practical benefits of increased clarity and ability to create a happier and more fulfilling waking life expand exponentially as well.

As it turns out, while Alice had not yet recalled an "unpainted strip" in a dream at the time of this book, she had had dreams about unfinished business -- dreams in which her dad was a main character. We'll tell you what she discovered when she used the PMID model with those dreams and how you, too, can easily expand your understanding of multiple dreams in the next section about dream series.

Although we have designed this book for self-facilitation, naturally the material is also applicable in clinical settings. So, in conclusion to these "PMID chapters" we present "Considerations for Dreamwork in Clinical Settings" next.

Considerations for Dreamwork in Clinical Settings

Eight similarities between dreaming and psychotherapy

(Revamped from an article by Ernest Hartmann "Making Connections in a Safe Place: Is Dreaming Psychotherapy?" *Dreaming, Journal of the Association for the Study of Dreams* 5(4), 1995, pp. 213-228.)

DREAMING
1. Dreams make connections between recent experiences and earlier memories. "Overall there is little question that . . . we appear to make distant connections or associations more easily during dreaming than during waking thought" (p. 215).
2. Dreams "often seem to be dealing with interpersonal problems, with the dreamer's current concerns about family, friends, lovers" (p. 215).
3. Dreams contain insights toward problem-solving solutions.
4. Dreaming provides a safe place for a trauma to be retold, associations to be made to related events, emergence of emotions, and gradual integration of emotions into the story until related stressful emotions diminish little by little.
5. If a trauma situation becomes chronic, dreams become repetitive.
6. Muscle paralysis of REM sleep refrains the dreamer from acting out.

7. Dreaming sometimes has the dreamer tell a story or read a story during the dream.
8. Dreaming is extreme free association. Self-criticism is relinquished automatically.

PSYCHOTHERAPY
1. Psychotherapy makes connections between recent experiences and earlier memories.
2. Psychotherapy deals with interpersonal problems about family and friends.
3. Problem-solving insights occur during psychotherapy.
4. Psychotherapy provides a safe place for a trauma to be retold, help in making associations to related events, encouragement to express emotions, gradual integration of emotions into the story until related stressful emotions diminish little by little.
5. If a trauma situation becomes chronic, psychotherapy often comes to a "stuck" place.
6. In psychotherapy, the client is helped to work through stress in ways other than "acting out."
7. One counseling technique has the client tell the story about distressful circumstances.

> 8. Free association is used in psychoanalysis and psychotherapy. The client is asked to relinquish self-criticism during the process.

Dreamwork and brief therapy

A psychotherapy that blends with use of the PMID model is Cognitive Behavior Therapy (expanded for dream interpretation). When people share emotional concerns with personal counselors, their dream recall often increases. The counselor's facilitation of the client's dreamwork could expedite the client's working through relationship issues. Brief therapy is highly used in personal counseling since brief therapy is central to most managed care behavioral health insurance plans that currently dominate the marketplace. The clear advantages of using dream interpretation during brief therapy include:

- Quickly build strong counselor-client working alliance;[39]
- Rapid identification of source of emotional distress by connecting dream to the dreamer's circumstances and associations;[40]
- Client ownership of dream contents and consequently ownership of responsibility for his/her role in conflicts depicted in dreams;[41]
- Identify solutions to problems.[42]

Dreamwork and distance counseling

---

[39] C. E. Hill. *Working with Dreams in Psychotherapy.* NY: The Guilford Press, 1996; C. E. Hill, et al. "A Structured Brief Therapy with a Focus on Dreams of Loss for Clients with Troubling Dreams and Recent Loss," *Journal of Counseling Psychology 47,* 2000, pp. 90-101.

[40] J. B. Hersh & E. B. Bynum. "The Use of Dreams in Brief Therapy," *Psychotherapy: Theory, Research and Practice 22*(5), 1985, pp. 248-254.

[41] J. B. Hersh & E. B. Bynum. "The Use of Dreams in Brief Therapy," *Psychotherapy: Theory, Research and Practice 22*(5), 1985, pp. 248-254.

[42] J. B. Hersh & E. B. Bynum. "The Use of Dreams in Brief Therapy," *Psychotherapy: Theory, Research and Practice 22*(5), 1985, pp. 248-254.

Distance counseling (especially asynchronous) is an excellent method to facilitate use of the PMID model. Clear advantages include:

- Clients' tendencies to express more freely when in non-inhibiting settings;
- Power of the written word to impel client and counselor to express themselves well;
- Virtual 24-7 flexible times for client and counselor input;
- Encourages self-exploration because clients are most often by themselves when writing/"talking"–putting dream information and insights into the distance delivery system;
- Expedites progress when client prepares information outside the usual 50-minute session;
- Opportunity for client and counselor to contemplate before responding;
- Opportunity for dream guidance intervening responses between counselors and clients;
- Ongoing "automatic" log of exchanges between client and counselor.

A caveat on bad or worrisome dreams

By now you have become aware that dreams and working with your own dreams can be powerful catalysts for understanding the deeper dynamics and realities of your emotional life, especially as it flows into the important parts of the lives of those we feel love, anger, jealousy, kinship, rivalry, pain, and joy within our most important moments. While these moments of insight and feeling usually have grounding and satisfying effects, we must also be aware that they can be disturbing at times on an intimate level.

When this occurs, it is important to consider exploring these feelings with others. That is, it may be useful to consult a professional counselor. Although not usual, this need does occur even with normal but highly stressful dreams. An example would be a dream series in which we wake up frightened or alarmed by what seems to occur repeatedly. This may be around an incident or trauma or tragedy that befell you or the family member. It may be about what seems to be a memory or fragment of a memory of something that is trying to come to the surface. It is important in these situations to remember that a dream may be emotionally true but not factually true. A dream may present a symbolic situation to you rather than an actual lived moment or series of past situations.

The unconscious is the great treasure house of not only our loves, hopes and expectations, but it also houses our primal fears, anxieties and social-cultural traumas that have not actually physically occurred to us but rather have impacted us on a psychological level. All the painful images painted each night on the nightly news of prisoner abuse, degradation and torture gives rise to a bottomless ocean of negative counter images in our collective dreams. Therefore, when you have negative and fearful dreams that repeat themselves, dreams in which you awaken repeatedly in a panic, or dreams in which there is a sickening sensation and a sense of foreboding and dread that follows you through the day, consider speaking with a professional counselor who is well versed in these intimate matters.

-Edward Bruce Bynum, Ph. D.

Section C

Dream Series

Introduction to Working with Dream Series

If you had a book about your life, would you be content to read only the first chapter? When you begin to interpret your nighttime dreams, you begin a book about your life. Would you be content with interpreting only one dream?

We live our waking lives in a wonderful and endlessly intertwined web of relationships and events. Once again, our dream world mirrors our waking world.

We have just completed an exercise interpreting a single dream that opened the door to a wealth of insight and understanding. Now imagine how much richer and meaningful this same dream would become if we knew about Alice's reactions to her dad in other dreams.

When you dedicate yourself to working with your dreams, you likely will soon notice more than one dream about a relationship or an issue. From our work with dreamers, we know it is very, very common to dream more than one dream about a relationship or issue. This is a *dream series*, in its simplest form.

The *series method* of interpreting dreams fits combinations of dreams together until the dreams fall into a meaningful picture of the dreamer.[43] Work with more than one dream is often critical to understanding our reactions to others, and, consequently, critical to understanding how to change our thoughts, attitudes and behaviors toward others when change seems beneficial. And, in the process we are able to follow our

---

[43] C. S. Hall. *The Meaning of Dreams*. Harper & Row, 1966.

psychological development over time[44] just as we do every day in our waking lives.

Additionally, relying on only one dream could be risky, especially for significant matters. Interpreting a series of dreams provides internal correctives to possible arbitrariness of a single dream interpretation.[45]

When more relationships than one are involved, you likely will find they become a kind of leitmotif in the living dream drama of your life, so it is naturally beneficial to work with more than one series of dreams. For example, a woman's dreams about a childhood friend, Carlie, revealed that her "Carlie-left-me-for-other-friends consciousness" also affected how she reacted to her husband (and to her other friends).

As the old saying goes, "You can't tell a book by its cover." Understanding a single dream certainly gives us a clearer understanding of our lives and selves, but it is comparatively somewhat similar to revealing only the cover or the first chapter. The dream series approach opens the whole book for us.

By making the effort to record more dreams using the PMID approach, the interpretation of each dream will become easier and easier because of the increasing wealth of information you will build about yourself and your dreams. You will start to recognize *your personal* common dream phrases and symbols meanings. Understanding the meaning of the dream becomes easier and more immediate as you begin to recognize familiar themes, events, and especially people and relationships during the course of your dreams.

In short, you are learning your own dream language. And, just like learning any other language, the more effort you make to understand it, the easier it will become. As we've said before, the best part is that it's mostly *your* language that *you* literally dream up for *yourself*.

As you read about the PMID process in the Section B of this book, no doubt you realized the PMID steps involve fundamental rules that are relatively easy to learn. Learning the PMID steps is a logical reasoning

---

[44] C. A. Jung, cited in J. A. Hall. *Clinical Uses of Dreams: Jungian Interpretations and Enactments.* NY: Grune & Stratton, Inc., 1977.
[45] C. A. Jung, cited in J. A. Hall. *Clinical Uses of Dreams: Jungian Interpretations and Enactments.* NY: Grune & Stratton, Inc., 1977.

process. *Applying* the PMID steps to your personal life is often largely an intuitive process.

As a final word of advice, many of your most significant learning, lessons, and breakthroughs will come from rather common dreams. Therefore, **it's important to *avoid focusing* on just your most dramatic or intense dreams,** just as you don't base your understanding of the people in your life solely on their most dramatic or wildest behavior.

We'll discuss frightening dreams in greater depth in Chapter 11. But, as much as these are often important dreams about a specific issue, by themselves they in no way give you a full or completely accurate understanding. In fact, you will learn much more from these "nightmares" by writing down and understanding your various more common dreams.

Note: All dreamers' words (Background, Dream and PMID steps) are in italics.

Chapter 8

Dreams about Parents

DAD
(Series that contains "Dad and the Inventory Dream")
Italicized Material by the Dreamer, Alice

Subsequent to Alice's "Dad and the Inventory" dream (shown in Section B), Alice looked closer at her other dreams about her dad. She found some earlier dreams that revealed unfinished business. While neither the earlier dreams nor the dreams after her "Inventory" dream contained the unpainted strip and the gray buildings that appeared in her "Dad and the Inventory Dream," the earlier dreams did contain symbolism for unresolved concerns. We present two of those earlier dreams and one subsequent dream, the last dream she presented in the series. First, Alice's background comments are shown.

Curiously, although I do not remember my dad ever telling me, "I love you," I have no recall of ever feeling that he did not love me or that he did not feel close to me. Sometimes I became very angry with him, though. Just the same, my best memory about my dad is that he often showed what I took as an above-average concern for my welfare. This first dream has my dad looking after me many years past his life on earth.

Alice's Dream Series: *My Dad Came Back for Me*

Dream: *It is early morning, still dark before the dawn. I am sleeping outside our family camper in a large camping ground that is like a parking lot. The campers are parked side by side.*

When I awake just before dawn, I notice our family camper is gone. They left and didn't realize I was sleeping outside.

I go up to a building. It seems like the community building hallway on the inside; only the hallway is longer. My dad is standing in the hall with several other people.

My dad has been looking for me. He looks tired. I knew he would come back for me. I look at him lovingly and have a good feeling about him.

Later he appears rested. He is dressed in a fine business suit with a very attractive tie with brown tones. He is young, slender and has a full head of hair, but I know it is my dad. He is talking to some people next to him. He tells them what hints to be a joke, but I believe he means it as a parable.

For the joke-parable, Dad takes some applesauce and spreads a thin line of it down the back of a man's tie. Then he spreads a thin line down the front of his tie. Then he says something like "you can tell a 'suck-up' person by what they will do." The man blushes, but goes ahead and licks the applesauce off the tie, starting at the bottom up.

PMID Step 1: Day-before-dream **event(s)** that connects to this dream.

Our family is on vacation at a campground. I fell asleep outside the camper on a lounge chair and dreamed this dream.

PMID Step 2: Day-before-dream **thought(s)** that connect to this dream.

This dream came before I recognized connections between day-before-the-dream thoughts and dream contents, so, regrettably, I did not consistently record day before the dream thoughts then.

Though I did not record pre-dream thoughts, I believe something must have happened the day before this dream that surfaced old thoughts and feelings of insecurity and inferiority, and then brought Dad into a dream to help me gain confidence and overcome feelings of inferiority.

Author: Although Alice did not record day before the dream thoughts, she did develop a theme from Step 1, events—*my unresolved reactions to Dad being humiliated*—on which to base her definitions of dream phrases and symbols in the next step, Step 3.

PMID Step 3: Major **dream phrases (and symbols)** defined in the context of this dream.

- ***Sleeping outside our family camper:*** *Searches my memory and sets up the messages of the dream. I began to be outside the family camp when I started talking to my dad about some of his behaviors several years ago.*

- ***Camping ground that is like a parking lot:*** *A much earlier experience that connects to my dream is that once when we were at the hometown community building and a man put my dad down, I went out to the parking lot where cars were parked side by side and sat in our car so I didn't have to watch Dad be humiliated.*

- ***Notice our family camper is gone:*** *Believe something must have happened the day before this dream that surfaced old thoughts and feelings of insecurity and inferiority, and left me feeling outside the family.*

- ***Left and didn't realize I was sleeping outside:*** *Whatever happened that resulted in my feelings of being left outside the family, wasn't something my family consciously did.*

- ***Go up to the building . . . seems like the community building hallway:*** *The community building is a place where my dad held a committee position for many years.*

- ***Dad is standing in the hall with several other people:*** *Hallway that led to where the community committees met. This scene reminds me of times when I was proud of my dad's accomplishments. My dad was on a major community committee for many years, a position he was dedicated to and proud of. I think my dream put Dad in that hallway to show he deserved respect.*

- ***Has been looking for me:*** *This dream shows my dad's concern for my feelings of belonging in the family group.*

- ***Looks tired:*** *Comes from looking for me. He has been looking for me from the time I began to "sleep outside the family camp."*

- ***Knew he would come back for me:*** *Though I became critical of my dad's actions at times, deep down I knew he has genuine concern for my wellbeing.*

- ***Later he appears rested:*** *This dream reveals my dad's genuine concern for me when he appears rested when he knows where I am.*

- ***Is dressed in a fine business suit:*** *Dad wears a self-confident personality. Clothes "as a rule represent levels of consciousness of the personality."*[46]

- ***Tells them [some people next to him] what hints to be a joke, but I believe he means it as a parable:*** *A parable is "A short allegorical story designed to illustrate or teach some truth" (Webster's Dictionary). I think Dad's parable is about getting over feeling inferior to others.*

- ***Takes some applesauce and spreads a thin line of it down the back of a man's tie:*** *Applesauce could point to "sass," which means "to speak impertinently or saucily to; sass" Webster's Dictionary). To answer back. (I did not know that one definition of "sauce" is "sass" before working with this dream.) My dad did answer back in the dream.*

- ***Man blushes, but goes ahead and licks the applesauce off the tie:*** *"Sucking up" to my dad, playing an inferior role to him.*

Author: Although Alice shares very little about having done something that put her "outside the family camp," she does reveal "*I began*

---

[46] J. Boushahla & V. Reidel-Geubtner. *The Dream Dictionary.* NY: Berkley Books, 1992.

to be outside the family camp when I started talking to my dad about some of his behaviors several years ago." What behaviors? Will another dream and her interpretations of it tell us more?

PMID Step 4: Dreaming **emotions** compared with waking life emotions.

The issue of this dream seems to be humiliation for Dad. I think something must have happened to me just before this dream that made me feel humiliated and inferior. I don't know, but whatever could have happened, in the dream Dad shows the opposite. He shows self-confidence.

My dreaming emotions toward Dad are "loving and a good feeling about him." My emotions about my dad when he passed on included anger.

PMID Step 5: Solutions or suggestions for changing thoughts, attitudes or behaviors (answer[s] to day-before-my-dream thoughts).

I think my dream suggests I need to "dress myself in confidence" (symbolized by my dad's fine clothes) and to answer back with self-confidence, at least to myself instead of cringing in feeling inferior to others.

PMID Step 6: Dreaming and waking life **reactions** to each person in this dream.

The main relationship in this dream is Dad. One systems effect shown in this dream that I might have taken on from my dad is acting inferior to others. I believe the dream is flipping some scenes I remember from my youth. My dad was inferior educationally and managerially to the better business people in the community. Nevertheless, there were times when some people unkindly put my dad down. I hurt for Dad when that happened. Because these people were community leaders, Dad must have felt he needed to have a high regard for them, no matter what.

Whatever his thoughts were, he seemed to cower to their power. Ironically, Dad often used the expression "inferiority complex" when he talked about another's personality. He was often boastful about himself. I have long recognized in myself at times the difficultly of quelling myself from boastful talking on the one hand and acting inferior on the other.

Author: Here in Step 6 Alice looks for further insights as to why her dad came in this dream. She also explores whether her reactions to him influence how she reacts in other relationship experiences, *the systems effect* we mentioned earlier. We can see Alice's interpretations definitely reflect systems effects from when she was younger.

Notice the above dream is actually more about systems effects than about her current relationship with her dad. Although he died several years ago, Alice receives valuable help from his presence in her dreams. Her dad comes with more help in this next dream.

Alice's Dream Series: *It is Done Within*

Dream: *It is dark and near midnight. My dad all of a sudden says, "I have to go to church," and says something about a message. We are in my parents' kitchen. The rest of the family is a little suspicious of Dad going to town, but I feel compassionate toward him. I ask him to whisper to me the message he heard. He whispers in my ear, to the effect, "It is done within."*

Dad is fearful. I think he believes it means he will be dying. At first, I think he might be right, but as I think about it, one word seems to tell me (if I understood his message correctly) it is good news. I tell Dad because of this word, it is good news. Yes, now it seems to him that it is good news, too.

A young woman, like Sharon Pope, says she is going to town, seems to church, too. That blends in with Dad saying he will go. . . . Mother, I believe, reminds Sharon she has to do her studies and has a test tomorrow. Sharon mumbles begrudgingly and leaves. . . .

Then we are all sleeping in the same bed in the kitchen, Mother and I and some of my siblings . . . a couple of my brothers.

I think of two red notebooks that would work for my portfolio. I get up and work on them. The inside paper binders have been separated from the first one that I work on. I drop the inside binders unintentionally. . . . That makes a noise and the brothers (in a bed here in this room, where I had been sleeping) complain. I look at the second folder. It also is missing the paper bindings. I go back to bed.

PMID Step 1: Day-before-dream **event(s)** that connects to this dream.

> *The event that connects most directly to the dream is at the time of the dream, including the day before this dream I am preparing a Personnel Portfolio, a "sales job" about my business accomplishments.*

Author: Looking back at the dream, we notice it isn't until near the end of the dream that Alice works on her portfolio, which connects with her waking life portfolio work. Still, that one clue gives the theme of this dream, what the dream is about -- *Work on my personnel portfolio*, and is the foundation for the rest of Alice's interpretations. Discovering the theme is that simple, as we will see during the rest of Alice's PMID work with this dream.

PMID Step 2: Day-before-dream **thought(s)** that connect to this dream.

> *The day before the dream, I was thinking how best to show myself in the portfolio.*

Author: Adding day-before-the-dream thoughts, we can see that the dream really zeroes in on the personnel portfolio. You might say, "Well, that thought is pretty obvious." Consider the various thoughts that you or others might have thought about the portfolio. "What a drag—This comes up every year." Or for a new employee, "What is a portfolio anyway? I've never prepared one before." Alice's ability to recall a specific thought that connects to her dream helps her understand what her dream answers.

She could even develop a thought-question when that seems fitting -- *"How shall I present my personnel portfolio to best represent me for purposes of my business position?"* Now she is equipped to develop her own unique experience-based meanings that relate to the dream phrases and symbols in this particular dream.

PMID Step 3: Major **dream phrases (and symbols)** defined in the context of this dream.

- **Dark:** *Inability to see how best to present myself in the personnel portfolio.*

- ***Near midnight:*** *Near a critical time for me to understand this message before it is time to submit my personnel portfolio.*

- ***Dad all of a sudden says, "I have to go to church":*** *In the setting of this dream, I believe means something other than a formal church. My dad usually only attended church with our family on special occasions. I believe the church in the dream perhaps represents inward reflection. When Dad all of a sudden says he must go to church, perhaps the dream suggests the suddenness of intuitive messages that come from within.*

- ***It is done within:*** *Inner-directed attention on one's self instead of needing attention from outer sources.*

- ***One word seems to tell me (if I understood his message correctly) it is good news:*** *Probably the word "within" from what my dad whispers to me, is the word that seems to tell me it is good news.*

- ***Sharon Pope says she is going to town, seems like to church, too:*** *Sharon is a very intuitive former classmate. At first, she failed to get the intuitive feel for the course material. Then it came in a flash for her.*

- ***Mother, I believe, reminds Sharon she has to do her studies and has a test tomorrow:*** *Notions my mother left on me that mental work, the studying, is more valuable than following one's heart desire.*

- ***All sleeping in the same bed in the kitchen, Mother and I and some of my siblings:*** *All sleeping in the same bed represents the same influences or beliefs. Yet, we are sleeping in the kitchen instead of our bedrooms. Here, the dream may remind me we have gone to sleep instead of doing the appropriate action in the place where we are. In the theme of this dream, needed to be up to work on my personnel portfolio.*

- ***Think of two red notebooks that would work for my portfolio:*** *Sometimes red indicates "attention-getting" activity to me. In this dream, the color red does mean attention-getting activity because the notebooks point to the personnel portfolio I am preparing.*

- *Inside paper binders have been separated from the first one that I work on:* Inner bindings, of the attention-getting red notebooks being missing, I believe, represent the "unbound" nature of the intuitive, in connection with the theme of this dream.

- *Drop the inside binders unintentionally. . . . That makes a noise and the brothers (in a bed here in this room, where I had been sleeping) complain:* My attempts to discover and use my inner intuitive nature causes a disturbance to my dominant nature–rational reasoning at the time of this dream.

- *Brothers:* I harmonize with the concept that all persons, male and female, have both masculine and feminine features in their minds. The masculine nature is the rational reasoning nature. The feminine nature is the intuitive, feeling nature.

- *When "The second folder . . . also is missing the paper bindings, I go back to bed":* In the dream I relent to my rational reasoning nature, and give up (go back to bed to sleep instead of continuing to prepare my Personnel Portfolio).

Author: As you read Alice's definitions of the above dream phrases and symbols, you likely will recognize she used universal-type meanings for a couple of them--darkness, brothers. Yet, she fashioned those universal-type meanings to her circumstances in this dream.

PMID Step 4: Dreaming **emotions** compared with waking life emotions.

Now during comparisons of dreaming and waking life emotions our dreamer wrote:

I do think dad's fearful feelings in the dream connect with my waking life anxiety about my work on the portfolio. However, in waking life before this dream, although I felt some anxiety on what to put in the portfolio, I certainly did not feel fearful.

In my dream, although the rest of the family are a "little suspicious of Dad going to town" I feel compassionate toward him. This is in contrast to how I most often felt in waking life about his frequent trips to town. Most times I felt very angry.

PMID Step 5: Solutions or suggestions for changing thoughts, attitudes or behaviors (answer[s] to day-before-my-dream thoughts).

This dream answers my yesterday's thoughts about preparing my personnel portfolio and suggests through the person of my dad that I must let go of needing approval from the outer, other people, for my feelings of self-worth. I should prepare the portfolio from my intuitive sense of my merits instead of preparing it from an irrational sense of needing others' attention to feel good about myself.

Let my inner intuitive nature be free (in my dream the binders are separated or missing). The message is, "It is done within." The dying is to the outer self. In my dream, I go back to bed, which I take to mean I yield to the rational reasoning dominance in my personality. Certainly, I do yield to rational reasoning in my waking life. It is scary to give up that dependence.

PMID Step 6: Dreaming and waking life **reactions** to each person in this dream.

Dad is a primary relationship in this dream. He represents himself and, in addition, represents desires that pull me toward the intuitive feeling part of my personality. I have resisted admitting that my emotional makeup resembles my dad's emotional makeup because, as a counselor once said, my dad let his emotions "run amuck." In the background of this dream, Dad's need for "outer approval" surely was behind some of his behaviors. The dream illustrates my dad's introspective intuitive nature, a nature I respect him for very much, though I did not notice him using that nature much.

Author: We see that the common event, preparing a personnel portfolio, gives Alice's dreaming mind an opportunity to bring in a wider perspective than just how to prepare the personnel portfolio. One major wider perspective is on her reactions to "dad's behaviors" that she referred to in her "Dad Came Back for Me" dream (above), behaviors that are revealed in this "It is Done Within" dream. (If she would have recalled her day before dream events and thoughts for her "Dad Came Back for Me" dream, she likely would have been able to derive even greater helpfulness from that dream.)

Recall that Alice's "Dad and Inventory" dream (Section B) answered her questioning thoughts about a specific circumstance: *"Am I still angry with my dad for unfair accusations of me when I was a teenager?"* Recall the answer she found in her "Dad and the Inventory" dream was she was no longer angry with him for being falsely accused. This helps us realize the importance of capturing the precise event(s) and thought(s) that bring a particular dream.

The next dream is the last dream of the sequence of dreams that Alice offered about her dad for this book. It is what we call a "settled" dream, meaning the dream shows the dreamer currently feels settled about most concerns she might have had from reactions to her dad.

Alice's Dream Series: *I Go Back to Dad*

Dream: *I am late for school. I am having difficulty with getting going, but I believe I will get there on time. There is something about the bus or other transportation. It is something about where it is.*

I start walking down the road past my parents' place, walking toward the next road. It is very dark. As I walk, I come by Dad who is on an old, old, simple weed-cutter type. There is a man way up front of Dad with another very simple old metal item of some kind. That item seems to be attached to Dad's weed-cutter. I see that they are getting some weeds cut, but, actually, the cutters don't cut the whole width of the swath.

In my hurry, I walk right on by, but I stop and turn around and go back to where Dad is. I tell him . . . I didn't mean to pass him by, and I stroke his arm in genuine compassion for him.

I walk on. I see the yellow of the bus in the distance, but I wonder how the driver will pick me up from here as the regular pickup place is at my parents' drive. As I continue trying to get to school, I see a "fast track," a runner rail where people get on and go in a hurry. The rails go in a sort of spiral time movement. That is the ticket; I'll go that way. I am pleased and excited.

PMID Step 1: Day-before-dream **event(s)** that connects to this dream.

The day before this dream, I told my husband about a book on dreams I am reading and told him I really like the book. There is a spiral picture accompanying one of the key dreams.

PMID Step 2: Day-before-dream **thought(s)** that connect to this dream.

Yesterday I thought about my mother discovering Dad had died in his sleep in bed. It was the first I had thought intensely about that. Then I thought about Dad dying "alone," and that I treated him coldly before he died when I was so angry with him about his "running after others" behaviors. I thought about Dad's attempts to give or did give a gift to me . . . and I was cold toward the gift. . . . I thought about that Dad must have felt tremendous pain from my anger toward him then.

One thought-question to which this dream may respond is "Is there any way I can possibly make up for having treated my dad so coldly during his later days on this Earth?"

Author: Adding her day-before-the-dream thought connections to her dream's meaning, we realize Alice's thoughts were far more serious than implied by the event she connects to her dream (seeing the spiral picture).

PMID Step 3: Major **dream phrases (and symbols)** defined in the context of this dream.

- ***Late for School:*** *Late to learn the lessons in this dream.*

- ***Having difficulty with getting going, but I believe I will get there on time:*** *Though I am late to learn the lessons in this dream, I still have confidence I will learn the lessons on time.*

- ***Start walking down the road past my parents' place:*** *Regular place to begin work with dreams about family, right where I was when my happenings with them came about. Dream shows my thought about needing always to go back home to learn more about my relationship with my parents, but that is not so.*

- ***Is very dark:*** *Symbolically, at this point in my dream, I cannot see the guidance this dream brings about my reactions to and relationship to my dad.*

- *Come by Dad who is on an old, old, simple weed-cutter type:* Dad is doing personality work, trying to cut the weeds that I thought smothered some of his flowering traits during this lifetime. Elementary method to do personality work.

- *Man way up front of Dad with another very simple old metal item of some kind:* Dad's father, whose ways of cutting weeds, of eliminating disturbing actions and thoughts, were very simple.

- *Item seems to be attached to Dad's weed-cutter:* Tools to cut out disturbing parts of the personality pass from generation to generation.

- *See that they are getting some weeds cut, but, actually, the cutters don't cut the whole width of the swath:* The generations who came before did work to weed out undesirable personality traits, and they did make progress, though their tools, their methods didn't eliminate the whole width of the swath, that is the whole scope of undesirable personality traits.

- *Walk right on by:* This scene reflects what I did do during my dad's later days on this Earth; I walked right on by my dad's feelings when I treated him so coldly.

- *But I stop and turn around and go back to where Dad is:* This is a response to a possible thought-question to which this dream may respond is "Is there any way I can possibly make up for having treated my dad so coldly during his later days on this Earth?" My dreams even before now picture him as a kindly helper to me and show my gratefulness for his "coming back for me". This current dream shows I have/am making up for having treated my dad so coldly during his later days on this Earth. I can "stop and turn around and go back to where my Dad is" while I am within a nighttime dream.

- *Tell him . . . I didn't mean to pass him by, and I stroke his arm in genuine compassion for him:* My dream reveals the true emotions I feel for my dad once I turn around and look for what he did do to overcome weed-like interferences in his life.

- ***See the yellow of the bus in the distance, but I wonder how the driver will pick me up from here as the regular pickup place is at my parents' drive:*** *Dream shows my thought about needing always to go back home to learn more about my relationship with my parents, but that is not so. One message in this dream is once I do go back and give compassion for him, I then am taken to a "fast track" onward.*

- ***See a "fast track," a runner rail where people get on and go in a hurry:*** *A way to hurry one onward, a way offered to me when I do go back and give genuine compassion to my dad. Oh, I deeply pray, my actions in this dream, do in some way "make up for having treated my dad so coldly during his later days on this Earth." This scene reflects my pre-dream reading of a book on dreams where there is a spiral picture accompanying one of the key dreams.*

- ***Rails go in a sort of spiral time movement:*** *Fast onward progress on relationship issues.*

- ***That is the ticket; I'll go that way:*** *Catch on to what this dream confers—because of my genuine compassion I express to my dad in my dreams, I can make onward rapid progress to overcome stress from relationship issues.*

PMID Step 4: Dreaming **emotions** compared with waking life emotions.

In my dream, I stroke my dad's arm in genuine compassion for him. I also have been feeling these compassionate emotions about Dad in my waking life. My dreams even before now picture him as a kindly helper and show my gratefulness for his "coming back for me." In this dream, I am pleased and excited about the fast track runner rail. In waking life, though I have realized my settled emotions about my dad lifted a heavy burden from me, I was unaware the degree this change in attitude could pave the way for "spiral" learning. Since the fast track comes after I go back to Dad, I wonder if fast track means having gone back to Dad and haven shown genuine compassion moves me rapidly onward in learning the lessons in this life.

Author: We see that Alice's dreaming emotions and waking life emotions about her dad are similar. There is a difference between her waking and dreaming realization of the possibility of fast learning resulting from showing compassion toward her dad.

PMID Step 5: Solutions or suggestions for changing thoughts, attitudes or behaviors (answer[s] to day-before-my-dream thoughts).

My dream answered my pre-dream thoughts [Step 2] *and possibly allowed me to do the solution right in my dream when I go back and let Dad know I care for him, the genuine attention that he so dearly wanted to regain. I wonder if Dad knows I did come back to him.*

The fast track seems to be at a place other than the end of my parents' drive, so I understand there is no need to go back to my earlier activities with them now. I now have the chance to start from a higher viewpoint for the next lessons in my life. Of course, the spiral symbol is from the book I read just before the dream; but I believe it does mean a move forward in the lessons of life, perhaps means in personality development because of my settled emotions about my dad.

Author: According to Maslow's Hierarchy of Human Needs, when physiological, safety, love and belonging, self-esteem needs are met it frees the person for self-actualization or self-development.

PMID Step 6: Dreaming and waking life **reactions** to each person in this dream.

The primary relationship in this dream is again, my dad. The man up front from Dad, I believe, is Dad's father who passed his "simple machine" ways on to his son, my dad. Dad did not have sophisticated tools for personality work when he walked the Earth; I must not hold him answerable as if he had a power mower. My waking life reactions to Dad before he died were to hold him answerable for actions I thought were highly questionable. "Judge not, that you be not judged"[47] was a favorite quote of his.

---

[47] Bible. *Matthew 7:1*, Possibility Thinkers New King James Version, edited by Robert H. Schuller. New York: Thomas Nelson Publishers, 1984.

Dad does continue to come in my dreams. I understand most of those dreams to mean I need to pay attention to my inner nature, something my dad seemed to have great difficulty doing, and something I have had difficulty doing.

Alice's added note: These are my dreams about my experiences with and reactions to relationships in my life. I readily realize others' personal experiences and reactions to any of the people in my dreams can only be understood by those others whose experiences are naturally different from my personal experiences.

Author: Systems effects -- reactions to others -- pass from generation to generation. Yet, these reactions are variable as well as improvable from generation to generation.

Father
Italicized Material by Dreamer, William

William's Dream Series: *Father Reappears Dream*

Dream: *The dream is a very long, involved and intricate story with multiple presences of family and extended family members. It occurs in a southern neighborhood like the neighborhood of my grandparents. The family of my sister's husband is involved. Also present are my mother, spouse, and others. There is not a clear "plot," mostly people relating to each other.*

I do have to pee, however, and am searching outside the houses for a private spot. After some sense of pressure and looking around, I find a place in an alley behind an older garage behind a house I know. When no one is looking, I prepare to pee quietly in the grass and earth.

Suddenly, my father appears and walks over to me with a male friend. My father is in a very good mood. He has lost some weight and is in a dark, formal suit. Not a tuxedo. He points at his stomach and gestures how good his body condition is. He has been in a hospital or something for a checkup and the report is very good. He smiles. I still need to pee, so they walk away toward the others who are around in front of the house. I awake and do actually use the bathroom.

PMID Step 1: Day-before-dream **event(s)** that connects to this dream.
Not certain what pre-dream events or thoughts connect to this dream since I, unfortunately, did not record those at the time of my dream.

Author: Since William, the dreamer, is uncertain of immediate events or thoughts that possibly connect with his dream, and did not offer a possible theme for his dream, we might be tempted to conjecture what might have been on his mind at the time of the dream, especially when we review William's work with the rest of the PMID steps. Yet, we remind you of the proviso that only the dreamer ultimately knows with a certainty what events or thoughts instigated this dream, so it is wise to leave the responsibility for coming up with a theme to the dreamer lest we mislead him.

PMID Step 2: Day-before-dream **thought(s)** that connect to this dream.

Not certain what pre-dream thoughts connect to this dream, since I, unfortunately, did not record those at the time of my dream.

PMID Step 3: Major **dream phrases (and symbols)** defined in the context of this dream.

- **Have to pee:** *I have to relieve myself of something. This is also objectively true!*

- **Searching outside the houses for a private spot:** *Looking for a quiet place to focus.*

- **Find a place in an alley behind an older garage behind a house I know:** *A familiar place, safe, secure.*

- **When no one is looking:** *I am alone, private.*

- **Prepare to pee quietly:** *I can focus myself, get close to nature.*

- **Father appears:** *Return of the dead to my life, since I know he is dead.*

- **Walks over to me with a male friend:** *My father is not alone. He has found help and support.*

- **Father in a very good mood:** *He was often grumpy, but now feels good!*

- **Lost some weight:** *Better health after his health issues -- his death!*

- **Dark, formal suit, not a tuxedo:** *Burial was formal occasion.*

- **Points at his stomach:** *This is where he lost weight and also "weight" around the heart.*

- ***Gestures how good his body condition is:*** *A transformation has occurred. Better now.*

- ***Has been in a hospital or something for a checkup:*** *The before death trauma is over.*

- ***Report being very good:*** *Optimistic about the future.*

- ***His smiles:*** *Good-natured now. No longer grumpy.*

PMID Step 4: Dreaming **emotions** compared with waking life emotions.
The dream felt calm and hopeful. My father was sometimes humorous, loud, teasing and critical. At other times grumpy, realistic, cynical and generous. Now he is at a deeper peace.

PMID Step 5: Solutions or suggestions for changing thoughts, attitudes or behaviors (answer[s] to day-before-my-dream thoughts).
I need to be more peaceful, accepting of my children's styles, less critical when they do not measure up to my own narrow standards. Be less grumpy myself.

PMID Step 6: Dreaming and waking life **reactions** to each person in this dream.
Primary person is my father. I am now a mature father who must continue to grow beyond my limits.

William's Dream Series: *Father Hug With Family, Plus The Door/Gate of Transformations*

Dream: *A convoluted and family drenched travel dream unfolds outdoors. I am with both my mother and wife in a wooded suburban area that also shifts or feels like the countryside. They are together on a porch. They mention that my father has had some kind of insight or change, which they are happy about.*
I walk over to where he is. He looks himself, but I am aware that he is deceased, I believe. However, this is ok. He hugs me, which is unusual for him. I am aware that

the two of them (my wife and my mother) are watching from a distance, so I subdue my surprise as I return the hug; then walk away. I wonder if I am to be like him in some way.

This scene smoothly flows into the next scene in which I am about to take a long trip with friends in a Winnebago. Somehow, a pet kangaroo is part of our journey. We travel to another country area that feels more mythological or allegorical in the sense that I am aware that we must travel "past" or "through" a door or gate. We talk and I speak to this gate/door, which is on the ground. I tell the gate/door and others that the gate/door is the door of death, and the land beyond it is real but unknown. There is a whisper of anxiety, but it is tolerable.

I say that the gate offers a gift to all travelers as the doorway from one world to another and that the worlds are endless through these gates of transformation. . . .

Somehow, resonance and vibration can resolve this dilemma.

PMID Step 1: Day-before-dream **event(s)** that connects to this dream.

My only recollection is that I was thinking about questions of science and how to approach them. Unfortunately, I did not record these at the time of the journal entry, only the dream itself.

PMID Step 2: Day-before-dream **thought(s)** that connect to this dream.

Again, I only recall thinking about certain scientific issues at the time. My journal entries did not include "pre-dream" events or thoughts that were not explicitly incorporated into the dream as direct images or relationships or events.

PMID Step 3: Major **dream phrases (and symbols)** defined in the context of this dream.

- **Wife and mother:** *Two closest women in my life, one a lover and companion, the other the "gateway" into this life for me, my mother.*

- **Feels like countryside:** *Outdoors, freedom and nature or natural real world.*

- **Father:** *Dead parent, source of many feelings, image of myself in the adult world. I am now a father myself.*

- **Hugs me:** *My father was not an openly affectionate man with his children, but he loved them. This is unusual for him, but he is "happy" about something now.*

- **Walk away from him:** *I feel awkward about others seeing me also express physical affection at times.*

- **A long trip:** *A journey of adventure or discovery.*

- **Friends in a Winnebago:** *A large comfortable room with friends.*

- **Pet kangaroo:** *Animal forces from the land "down under!"*

- **Travel to a mythological country:** *Travel to a surreal place beyond the natural, outdoor countryside world I know. Dream-life.*

- **"Past" or "through" a door:** *A transformational journey, beyond my current understanding.*

- **Speak to this door:** *I talk to death and transformation itself!*

- **Whisper of anxiety:** *I am apprehensive, but contain my fear and summon my course.*

- **Resonance and vibration:** *Somehow, science and meditation or a disciplined science of meditation is the pathway through transformation.*

PMID Step 4: Dreaming **emotions** compared with waking life emotions.

The dream reflects my primary concerns, pre-occupations, anxiety and searchings while also expressing my emotional loss of my father and the complicated feelings of that relationship. I still feel awkward expressing and receiving affection from him. He was not a physically affectionate man to his sons in life and was demanding of them (while still being loving). I have struggled with that set of feelings. Also, my quest to find the discipline of mind and spirit to transform myself is bound up in this. His death deepened my search into all this. I struggle to approach death as a pathway of transformation into the deeper mysteries of spirituality and the soul. My courage is usually there, but sometimes threatens to fail me, and I fear I may sink into anxiety.

PMID Step 5: Solutions or suggestions for changing thoughts, attitudes or behaviors (answer[s] to day-before-my-dream thoughts).

I will <u>not</u> give in to anxiety, fear or awkward feelings, but, instead, will persist. The outcome is both ultimately some "insight," "happiness," and the art or science of gateway/door passage and transformation.

PMID Step 6: Dreaming and waking life **reactions** to each person in this dream.

There are three: my father, my wife and my mother. I must find myself in all of these. All are my teachers in some way on this life's journey, a journey that will go on even into "the land down under" and beyond.

Mama
Italicized Material by Dreamer, Eleanor

Background: *My mama's influence on me was huge. It was huge longing for her; it was huge hurting for her; it came to be huge dislike of her; it came to be huge joy for her. It now is huge compassion and love for her. She was a fine woman. I wish she had known that!*

Mama never hurt me bodily, never laid a hand on me in punishment, and she never said mean things to me. I didn't know "out loud" she had trouble feeling close to me. ... I did know inside, hidden from me really, that it seemed Mama liked boys better than girls. I think my dreams, when I don't know who the child is, and the child is a boy, means I think of me as a boy child.

Author: We tell you up front that Eleanor had a very difficult time to understand this first dream. It was only after she dreamed her "Mama Pushes a Woman Back Who Was Trying to Help Her" (the dream that follows this dream) that Eleanor finally understood the meanings to her "My Suitor Who Did Not Suit Mama" dream.

Eleanor's Dream Series: *My Suitor Who Did Not Suit Mama*

I am in a room with Captain, our children's dog. At some time, I know the room is my parents' kitchen. Mama is here, but she pays us no mind.

I am awestruck with Captain; it is not a physical sexual feeling; it is just a deep love and compassion for him. He is standing upright and is wearing a very deep blue suit. ... Captain and I hug each other and dance around a bit. I faintly know Mama is not at all interested in our love for each other.

I know Captain must go outside. I follow him to the door. There's a snowstorm going on outside and I fret about him, but I think, dogs do know how to take care of themselves outside.

I watch him as he walks away. I specially notice his blue suit as it covers his shoulders and back. I fret the suit is getting wet. I call after Captain to go somewhere to keep warm and I picture him curled up and comfortable.

PMID Step 1: Day-before-dream **event(s)** that connects to this dream.

A couple of nights before this dream, a pro-basketball coach caught my eye as he walked off the floor at half-time, especially his deep blue suit coat and the cut of it across his shoulders. Not when I had this dream, but later I came up with the theme of this dream as "my identity as a woman."

Author: Eleanor easily made the connection -- deep blue suit on the dog in the dream -- and deep blue suit on the coach in waking life was wearing, but she had a difficult time to understand the message of the dream. It was sometime later before Eleanor came up with a theme of her dream as *"my identity as a woman."* Hmmm, well we will keep the rest of the story for later.

PMID Step 2: Day-before-dream **thought(s)** that connect to this dream.
Nothing I know of.

PMID Step 3: Major dream **phrases (and symbols)** defined in the context of this dream.

- ***Captain, our children's dog:*** *Our children's dog that we loved. I often said, "Captain doesn't know he is a dog. He thinks he is a human."*

- ***Know the room is my parents' kitchen:*** *The door to my parents' kitchen was the entryway into the house. When people came to visit, in this dream, Edward, they came to the kitchen door.*

- ***Mama is here, but she pays us no mind:*** *Mama paid no mind to whether Edward and my friendship was of any good.*

- ***Standing upright and is wearing a very deep blue suit:*** *The suit the basketball coach wore when I watched him walk off the floor a couple of nights before my dream. The coach's figure is a lot like a former boyfriend of mine, Edward.*

- ***Faintly know Mama is not at all interested in our attraction for each other:*** *Mama disapproved my liking Edward's attention.*

- ***Know Captain must go outside:*** *Takes me back to a scene when Edward walked out the door after I broke off with him. He had to be treated like a dog, not a human.*

- ***A snowstorm going on outside:*** *No recall of a snowstorm, did seem like a storm treatment to send a person away who had treated me good.*

- ***Think, dogs do know how to take care of themselves outside:*** *Well, I did know Edward could well take care of himself, even when treated like a dog.*

- ***Specially notice his blue suit:*** *Another reminder of the suit the basketball coach wore when I watched him walk off the floor a couple of nights before my dream. The coach's figure is a lot like a former boyfriend Edward.*

PMID Step 4: Dreaming **emotions** compared with waking life emotions.

My dreaming emotions tie to emotions I felt about a person who had to be treated like a dog. I was awestruck by Edward's attention to me, but Mama treated him like a dog. In the dream and in waking life I turned my joy at being a woman out in the snow, the cold.

Deep compassion for him (Captain) in my dream, but I can't see how this ties to my feelings about Edward, because I didn't grieve much for him after he left. Looking back, I think my dream's deep compassion is what I felt for me who liked being treated like a woman, an attractive woman. In waking life, I haven't realized I was missing these emotions about me, the woman.

Author: Notice the hidden emotions that show up in a dream. This idea of love of self, love of enjoying being a woman did not escape the dream, the dream that reached to emotions further than Eleanor's waking cognitions would allow. This is a good example of how comparing dreaming emotions with waking life emotions can better clarify the meaning of a dream.

PMID Step 5: Solutions or suggestions for changing thoughts, attitudes or behaviors (answer[s] to day-before-my-dream thoughts).

I believe the dream shows I still react from Mama's turned off attitude toward me, the woman, when something clicks my memory, of liking to be treated as a woman, an attractive woman, like Edward did.

Another thing, this dream came when I was feeling much lack of respect from Mama for being a woman. Read my Mama dreams to find out when she finally recognizes me as a woman.

Author: So, we see the dreamer interprets *"miss the feelings I had when I gloried in being a woman"* instead of breaking a relationship with a person who gave Eleanor "Elvis Presley-like attention" still causing a problem.

PMID Step 6: Dreaming and waking life **reactions** to each person in this dream.

The primary relationship in this dream is Mama. Edward, a former boyfriend is another one. Edward was an Elvis Presley type "romancer" who liked attractive women. I felt flattered when he liked me. Looking back, I know it was I liked being treated special because I was a woman. I can't think I would have ever married Edward, but Mama's disapproval of him was the reason I broke off when I did.

Eleanor's Dream Series: *Mama Pushes a Woman Back Who Tried to Help Her*

Mama is in a little room and a woman goes in to help her. For no reason at all, Mama shoves the woman back away from her. The woman does not understand. I know it is because Mama has trouble with liking women.

PMID Step 1: Day-before-dream **event(s)** that connects to this dream.

I worked hard for a long time before I came to the meanings of my "My Suitor Who Did Not Suit Mama" dream. One night after I had worked hard about the meaning of my Suitor dream, I had this dream.

Theme of this dream is "my identity as a woman."

Author: We trust you find the connections to this dream much easier than to Eleanor's Suitor dream. We simply connect Eleanor's day before the dream "work on Suitor dream" with the message in the dream, "Mama has trouble with liking women" to understand the theme in this dream again is *my identity as a woman*. So, let's see what thoughts Eleanor had about her work with the suitor dream.

PMID Step 2: Day-before-dream **thought(s)** that connect to this dream.

Last night as I worked again on the Suitor dream, I thought, this is really hard and I mulled over trying to come up with what that dream could really mean.

Author: We remind you that Eleanor only came to the meanings she developed for her prior "Suitor" dream *after* she dreamed this "Mama Pushes a Woman Back" dream. A wonderful aspect of working with dreams is that not only do dream messages repeat themselves, as we have seen with Eleanor's "identity as a woman" message, but dreams also build on each other. That is, when we work intensely to understand one dream, another dream could come to help us understand the first dream, as this one did!

PMID Step 3: Major **dream phrases (and symbols)** defined in the context of this dream.

- ***Woman goes in to help her:*** *This happened lots of times when Mama was being cared for.*

- ***No reason at all, Mama shoves the woman back away from her:*** *Yep, Mama pushed women who helped her away. Shows Mama's low respect for women.*

- ***Woman does not understand:*** *Sure, she doesn't know Mama has trouble to take help from women.*

- ***Know it is because Mama has trouble with liking women:*** *All righty! That's why Mama was cold toward my being liked for being an attractive woman in my Suitor dream.*

Author: See the very simple dream picture that brought a tremendous new insight.

PMID Step 4: Dreaming **emotions** compared with waking life emotions.

In my dream, I recognize Mama has difficulty with women, but I didn't record any emotions about that. In my waking life, I just didn't think about Mama's problem with women coming down to have bearing on how she felt about me, so I don't know my emotions about that.

PMID Step 5: Solutions or suggestions for changing thoughts, attitudes or behaviors (answer[s] to day-before-my-dream thoughts).

I think the dream just plain shows I need to recognize Mama pushing me away from closeness to her came from something she needed to fix, not something I did wrong.

PMID Step 6: Dreaming and waking life **reactions** to each person in this dream.

Of course, Mama is the main relationship here. For some reason, Mama did not show liking for women or treat them with the same respect she had for men. She had very few women friends. I think this dream shows I let Mama's low respect for women shape my respect for me as a woman, which helps me figure out the Suitor dream, specially since I worked on it the night before this dream.

Liking my womanliness is my job. It doesn't depend on an Edward, whom I did not love enough to marry, and it doesn't depend on my husband, who really shows more love for me than any other suitor I ever had.

Mama never "danced" with me or hugged me that I remember before the last five years of her life. Of course, I don't think she made an on-purpose effort to push me away. Something must have happened in her life to push her away from women. I feel for her now when I think of the weight her coldness to women must have been for her.

I wonder if some of my actions toward Mama came from down deep trying to keep her from pushing me away. I know I attached myself to her, and showered super attention on her.

Author: As we examine the systems' effects that the dreamer finds in these dreams, we notice almost ripple effects from the mother to the daughter, even to a former boyfriend. From there, it could go to the daughter's children, friends. ...

We have no idea at this point what happened to cause Eleanor's mama such difficulty in liking women, and we don't need to know. We do need to know the importance of understanding when we are living our lives, living our dreams, instead of living someone else's life void of dreams.

Next is another dream that shows Mama's liking boys more than girls. Pretty shocking when it came about, and its honesty.

Eleanor's Dream Series: *Mama Named Her Second Child "Barry"*

It is a little dark in here. Mama has been talking with us. ... There are lots of things; it is not orderly here; it is cluttered.

I know Mama has brought home her second child, but no one has asked about it. When I'm alone with Mama, I think about the babe, and realize he is covered up and is among the clutter in the kitchen. He is in a baby carrier covered by denim cloth and probably he has denim on. I don't see him with my eyes, but I see him in my mind's eye.

I say, "Oh, Mama, about the baby, I want to see him," and "Oh, what an appropriate name, Barry!"

PMID Step 1: Day-before-dream **event(s)** that connects to this dream.

The greatest tie in the dream to my waking life events is the day after Mama died (two months before this dream), and I was working at a day-care center. I wasn't aware I was calling one of the children by the wrong name until he asked me if I was calling him "Barry." His name is Gary.

I did not know why I said the name Barry until the morning after this "Barry" dream when I laid down and sort of silently asked, "Why the name Barry?" The thought quickly came, Barry -- Gary , B is for boys and G is for girls! My mouth dropped open I was so shocked. It does fit my idea of myself as B for boys instead of G for girls.

Also in my minute meditation, I asked, "Why was the child in the dream the second child?" Oh! I am the second child. . . . In the dream, I am a boy as shown by the new babe Mama has brought home, the second child.

PMID Step 2: Day-before-dream **thought(s)** that connect to this dream.

Author: None recorded, so we are unsure what thoughts could have prompted this dream. Eleanor did have some powerful insights from her "minute meditations" after this dream. She used those insights to help her define some of her dream phrases and symbols.

PMID Step 3: Major **dream phrases (and symbols)** defined in the context of this dream.

- ***Little dark in here:*** *Something I don't see clearly.*

- ***Is not orderly here; it is cluttered:*** *Some ideas are cluttering up my mind from childhood. Mama was a fine housekeeper, but I think cluttered in this dream means my "favorite sons idea" about Mama was still cluttering up my mind after Mama died. Favored-sons idea comes from I unawares pictured myself as a boy because I unawares thought Mama preferred boys. My dream does one of those "telling on me" things here.*

- ***Know Mama has brought home her second child:*** *Me. I am Mama's second child.*

- ***But no one has asked about it:*** *It could be nobody asks because he is something not talked about. I never talked about my favorite sons idea when I was younger, maybe never thought about it myself. My dream gives me a chance to ask Mama about it.*

- ***When I'm alone with Mama, I think about the babe, and realize he is covered up and is among the clutter:*** *Just maybe* *"alone with Mama" means alone with my thoughts about Mama after she died and still thinking about her two months later.*

- **Is in a baby carrier covered by denim cloth and probably he has denim on:** *Sign of child's sex. When I was growing up men and boys were the ones who mainly wore denim.*

- **Don't see him with my eyes, but I see him in my mind's eye:** *The dream shows the idea that I must be a boy is in my mind, not actual in my waking life.*

- **Say, "Oh, Mama, about the baby, I want to see him," and "Oh, what an appropriate name, Barry!":** *Barry is the name I mistaking called a little boy the day after Mama died. His right name is Gary.*

PMID Step 4: Dreaming **emotions** compared with waking life emotions.
I didn't record emotions about Mama in this dream, but I see no hints of bad feelings towards her.

PMID Step 5: Solutions or suggestions for changing thoughts, attitudes or behaviors (answer[s] to day-before-my-dream thoughts).
This dream shocks me into knowing I still see me as a little boy. I know now why I mixed up the child's name two months before this dream, the day after Mama died. I had mixed up the B (for boy) instead of G (for girl) because of my strong thoughts about Mama. I hadn't made that mistake with the child before that I remember. I take it from this dream I'd better do something about seeing me as a boy, since I am a girl, a woman.

I wonder what would have happened if I had known I was dreaming and had asked Mama about the babe. I wonder what she would have told me. Just the same, my dream gave me the answer with the name Barry and the second child. Mama didn't need to tell me.

PMID Step 6: Dreaming and waking life **reactions** to each person in this dream.

I don't know just what happened in Mama's life that she had such trouble feeling close to women. I do think her low respect for women swayed some of my choices. Up until about ten years ago, I favored men employers and friends. The first job I chose was thought of as a man's job.

A waking twist of fate is sometime after this dream, someone who didn't know about the dream and didn't know anything about Mama and my relationship gave a sweatshirt to me. The sweatshirt is pink. (Mama would only wear pink the last few years of her life. She said, "Pink is for girls." Did Mama miss being a little girl, too?) There is a company name printed across the front of the sweatshirt. The name printed on my pink sweatshirt is "Barry's, Inc."

Author: To what extent the mother's influence had on Eleanor's choices, we do not know. We do know it had the potential for at least some influence. This is not to say it is necessarily a bad thing that Eleanor feels more comfortable with male employers and friends. It is helpful for her to be aware of when she makes decisions about employers and friends. The larger concern is about how she identifies herself.

We will tell you that Eleanor does have dreams (not shown here) where she identifies herself as a girl. Her comment: "Yea! The child is a girl!"

This next dream shows quite a change in my emotions about life with Mama. I dreamed it a couple of months after my "Mama Named Her Second Child, 'Barry'" dream.

Eleanor's Dream Series: *Mama's Dark Sun Glasses*

I am standing in front of the china kitchen cabinet in my childhood house. It is a little like dusk in here. I'm looking at something of Mama's laying inside the bottom self on the right side on top of something; it is a pair of dark sunglasses, sort of elaborate somehow.

Mama has just died, and I'm the only one left in the house. I think about how I'll be selling these things. I think about how all of the others have gone and I'm the only one in the family still living at home. I feel a faint deep quiet joy as I let a little thought come in about how I can now make the decisions about the house.

PMID Step 1: aa**nt(s)** that connects to this dream.

I have been coming into alertness, much more, of the spiritual area. Last night I even felt like I am a different person. This is a quiet thing, sort of ahead of my doing. Still I oblige, or don't oblige, as it moves and operates. I believe that ties to this dream when the dream shows I know I have control of my childhood house and the things in it, which I think goes to control of my childhood thoughts that are in my mind.

It was just a little more than four months ago that Mama died.

Author: As we have seen, the first clue to understanding a dream is the theme. For this dream, the theme Eleanor chose is *control over my thoughts about Mama's influence.* That clue comes from connecting waking life "last night I even felt like a different person" and "four months ago Mama died" to the dream events of "can now make decisions about the house," and "Mama has just died."

PMID Step 2: Day-before-dream **thought(s)** that connect to this dream.

My thoughts were about realizing I am succeeding in coming into higher well-being feelings.

Author: Eleanor digs deeper into why she had this dream when she connects her last night's thought about her "higher well-being feelings" to her dream. We can look at that thought as a question that her dream answers. Though not her actual thought, translated into understanding how dreams function, a possible thought question could have been, "What helps me be aware of those 'higher well-being feelings'"?

PMID Step 3: Major **dream phrases (and symbols)** defined in the context of this dream.

- ***Standing in front of the china kitchen cabinet in my childhood house:*** *Shows the dream ties to my childhood home.*

- ***Little like dusk in here:*** *Something in this dream isn't clear to me, in the first of this dream at least.*

- ***Dark sunglasses, sort of elaborate somehow:*** *Seeing things elaborately dark. I've thought these were Mama's dark and elaborate sunglasses, specially since they were left in her house. She did come to seeing happenings darkly. All the same, I sure need to keep from seeing her part in my life darkly.*

- ***Mama has just died, and I'm the only one left in the house:*** *My childhood memories are mine to take care of. No one else is here to take charge of those memories.*

- ***Selling these things:*** *Getting rid of any old thoughts and feelings that don't help me.*

- *Think about how all of the others have gone and I'm the only one in the family still living at home:* Probably "I'm the only one" points right at me and to these being my dreams and my story about Mama's place in my life. So it's my job to get rid of any old thoughts and feelings about Mama that don't help me.

Author: These make it easier to understand personal experiences behind Eleanor's relationship with her mother, but we need a little more help from Step 4.

PMID Step 4: Dreaming **emotions** compared with waking life emotions.

In my dream, I have faint deep quiet joy about being able to make the decisions about the house. In waking life, as I said, I am succeeding in coming into higher well-being feelings. I know, more now than ever, I do have some control over my thoughts and over how I feel about things. When I connect this to Mama, who this dream talks about, I can believe my feeling so well in the dream goes along with my waking life higher well-being feelings about my life with Mama.

PMID Step 5: Solutions or suggestions for changing thoughts, attitudes or behaviors (answer[s] to day-before-my-dream thoughts).

To me this dream shows one thing that helped me have higher well-being feelings is that I realized deep down first, I suppose, and then in waking life, that I can control my thoughts about my life with Mama. I don't have to be dark-looking about whatever happened.

Maybe this dream shows times when Mama thought darker thoughts. In my opinion, she took some of the things that happened to her so hard it got to where she looked for something bad to talk about before looking for something good to talk about. Mama's dark sunglasses in the dream maybe hint at my still needing to get over thinking down about some things. Because I decide what I think, I do have control, so I can decide to throw the dark sunglasses away.

Author: Notice this dream does reflect successful thought modifications. For one, Eleanor is not now in a cluttered room, as she was in the dream about Barry.

PMID Step 6: Dreaming and waking life **reactions** to each person in this dream.

Mama had a lot of troubles in her life. Anyway that is the way I saw it. This dream made me remember before Mama's happenings began looking dark to her, before she put on the elaborate dark-colored glasses, her dogged "looking-up" way of thinking often saved her from worrying thoughts. I want very much to trash seeing my past, present or future in dark-colored ways. I want very much to put on only looking up glasses.

Chapter 9

Coincidence of Psi-dreams of Marital Pair -- Same Night Dreams

Husband's Dream

I dreamed that my youngest brother, my older sister, and an unidentified man were all near the bank of a river whose current was increasing in intensity. The bank was at the curve of the river, and I was aware of the current getting stronger and stronger.

Suddenly, as my sister was farther away down the riverbank and the unidentified man held my brother above the water, as if to bathe him or help him swim, the slowly rising river current coming around the bend swallowed him and took him underneath the current. I was beside myself with grief. I called out to "the Living One" for help, but my brother did not re-emerge from the water.

PMID Step 1: Day-before-dream **event(s)** that connects to this dream.

As I recall this was a time in our (my wife and my) relationship in which we talked a lot about having children.

PMID Step 2: Day-before-dream **thought(s)** that connect to this dream.

As I recall this was a time in our relationship in which we were intensely debating (thinking about) a child and when to have the child.

PMID Step 3: Major **dream phrases (and symbols)** defined in the context of this dream.

- ***Near the bank of a river:*** *Near life flowing, waves of feelings.*

- ***Current increased in intensity:*** *Life and feeling getting deeper and more serious.*

- ***Curve of the river:*** *Twists and turns of life and fate.*

- ***Current getting stronger and stronger:*** *Sense of being overwhelmed, loss of control.*

- ***Sister farther away down the riverbank:*** *My sister did not have children, farther away.*

- ***Unidentified man holding my brother above the water:*** *Helpful ancestor to us.*

- ***As if to bathe him or help him swim:*** *Baptizing in river of life, sanctify.*

- ***Suddenly the river current swallowing him:*** *Sudden twist of fate, loss of control, swallowed by death.*

- ***Taking him underneath the current:*** *Below the surface, underworld.*

- ***Brother not re-emerging from the water:*** *Death and loss.*

- ***Calling out to "the Living One" for help:*** *The God of all life and light beseeched.*

PMID Step 4: Dreaming **emotions** compared with waking life emotions.

In my dream, I was beside myself with grief. Waking life feelings were good but diffuse. This is the loss of one stage or period of my life, a kind of spiritual death, but uncertainty about the future emergence.

PMID Step 5: Solutions or suggestions for changing thoughts, attitudes or behaviors (answer[s] to day-before-my-dream thoughts).

This was the emotional topic of the time: deeper commitment, death of former self, acceptance of new role (fatherhood), grief of losing youth to a new life.

PMID Step 6: Dreaming and waking life **reactions** to each person in this dream.

Primary relationship: Younger brother who I was care-taking for and guardian. He also represents innocence of youth, vulnerability and dependence on me. I have tender memories of his youth and his trust in me.

Wife's Dream

I was bathing a child, not my own, in a bathtub. Suddenly, the child slipped from my hands and went under the water. I was startled for a few seconds, and then reached for the child. My hands were weak, but I did manage to re-emerge the child from the water.

Author: Wife does not recall this dream several years later. Luckily, the husband who keeps a dream log wrote it down in his journal at the time he recorded his same night dream. At the time of this dream, the couple noted similarities in their same night dreams: *"In both cases there was a male child, not our own child by birth, who either fell or was lost under the water. We were both startled."*

Chapter 10

Galen's Dreams Snatches about Victorious Handling of Situations

Galen offered a unique series of dreams, most of which are about situations that, in turn, affected his reactions to others. The first dream Galen volunteered though is about a specific person.

Ruffians Living With Me

Dream: *My wife went someplace for some time -- maybe two weeks or a month -- I don't know how long. Some people came and lived with me while she was gone. They were kind of ruffians, and I was concerned that they would not leave before my wife came back.*

Background: *Yesterday I worked out in the back part of our acreage doing some tractor work. My wife came out a couple of times just to see how things were going for me. I appreciated that and told her so. I thought about times in the past when she has been away from home and I felt concerned about her devotion to home. Those were "rough" (Ruffians) times.*

Won the Game in the 13th Inning

Dream: *I was playing softball. Seems like in high school . . . seems like it was in the first inning and we got behind. May have fallen behind a few or more runs, but later we catch up.*
Then it was in the 9th inning, but that seems more like baseball, because of the 9th inning. Anyway, it was softball and in the 9th inning. Then the other team scored four runs. In the bottom of the 9th we scored four runs to tie it up. So the game went into extra innings.

Then in the 13th inning either I walked and stole second and someone else hit me in, or someone else walked and stole second and I hit him in to score the winning run. . . . This was the bottom of the 13th, so we won the game.

Background: *Our plans for the day before this dream changed when a young kid ran into our vehicle and some farm work we planned turned out to be a bigger job than we could do ourselves. I filled out the required report for the accident, and since we were unable to do the bigger job, had time to accomplish several smaller jobs we hadn't anticipated having time to do. I guess we "won the game in the 13th inning" in the face of some circumstances that could have seemed unlucky, if we had fretted over them.*

False Judgment of Myself

Dream: *Someone has filed a judgment against me. It is obviously false. The judgment is false.*

Background: *Yesterday my wife cautioned me about putting myself down. Maybe my dream shows that I did drop my false judgments against myself yesterday.*

Escape from Kidnappers

Dream: *I was kidnapped. They didn't harm me though. I finally somehow was able to call 9-1-1 and some people came and I got away from the kidnappers.*

Background: *The dream could come from my feeling in bit of a down mood yesterday and some the day before. At the end of the day yesterday, I was successful in changing my attitude to more upbeat. I think my dream shows the escape I made from feeling a bit down during the day.*

Top Flight of Runners in an Obstacle Course

Dream: *I was back at Clearwater. It was in the country someplace and I was involved in some kind of obstacle course. I became hung up on some briars and thorns. I thought there were unnecessary delays, "obstacles." But the person in charge said, "You have only been on the course 4½ minutes, something like 4 or 4½, and you are in the top flight of the fastest runners."*

Background: *Yesterday everything I worked on seemed to have some kind of hassle to it. I kept on working, though. Guess my dream shows I actually accomplished more than I thought I had. Maybe it is talking about my having kept on even in the face of discouragement yesterday.*

Doing "Foolish" Things Keeps People Going in Stressful Times

Dream: *There were kids who were just driving around the town. People were suspicious of what else they may be doing, but that is all they were doing was driving around the town.*

Background: *Last night I watched the MASH TV program about stress and tension in the camp because of the demands and the intensity of the circumstances, and Sidney, the psychologist came into camp. Then it turned out from putting infected clothes in a pile to burn, people put other things on to burn. Col. Potter ordered them to stop before they burned up these other things, and Sidney, says, "You know maybe this is what they need to do, maybe this will relieve the stress." Col. Potter said to go ahead and they threw stuff on until they had a huge fire going. They were doing foolish things, which relieved tension.*
My wife and I have been feeling stress between us from thinking differently about one of our kids. People do foolish things; they just do. That may be the thing that keeps them going -- doing these foolish things. Maybe my dream is saying to us to "do some foolish things" to relieve the tension.

Field of Dreams at the End of a Struggle Journey

Dream: *This seemed like a repeat of other dreams. I am first on a good road and traveling along, the roads go into worse and worse roads to travel. Finally, I come to a tunnel and go through that. Then, I finally come to a scene that looks like the photo I saw last night of the farm where the movie, "Field of Dreams," was filmed.*

Background: *Last evening I read an article touting the state of Iowa. The picture on the first page of the article is a large air shot of the whole Field of Dreams at Dyersville, Iowa. The article and the picture brought my spirits up from having felt discouraged. However, I'm curious as to what going through the tunnel means. It is a hopeful sign to me.*

Taking Care of Old Business

Dream: *Seems like I was retired and they called me back to work for just a day or a day and a half. There were things that had not been taken care in a long time and I was there to tell them to get those things taken care of.*

Author: Galen had no idea what the dream could mean. He did share his wife's comments about the dream: "Yesterday Galen made a special day of it, being the anniversary of the day we were engaged. He also worked on the tailpipe and muffler of our car, and although there were discouraging things that happened with repairing the muffler, Galen kept up a fine attitude. Although it appeared that we might have lost a wire cutter in the fields, Galen expressed no agitation of that at all. What unfinished business was Galen thinking about yesterday? Could it be taking care of reactions to things -- his attitude is so noticeably fine."

Blowing Off Steam

Dream: *There is a fellow who let gas and the gas blew with such force that it blew a small hole -- perhaps the size of a dime -- in his underpants. Then he let another gas blow and this time it blew a hole in his outer pants -- still a small sized round hole.*

However, if the two holes become lined up others could see clear into his nakedness. So, he got some tissue and patched the holes up.

Background: *Yesterday a friend and I argued. Then last night a windstorm came through our area, and made me think how destructive "wind" can be. My dream could be showing that even if it might help to blow off steam, excessive "windy" blowing off steam could result in revealing parts of me I am unwilling to reveal.*

Key that Fits Two Cars

Dream: *I went someplace with Gertrude. I was driving. Don't know where we went and don't know what we did. But when we got back, someone said that we had driven the wrong car back. There was a Mercedes and a Chevrolet and we drove one of them to wherever we went, and drove the other one back. We were very confused as to how one key could have fitted both cars.*

Background: *Gertrude is a relative on my side of the family. She has difficulty getting along with several of the other relatives. Somehow, though, she has been receptive to my friendly attitude toward her -- doesn't seem to be disagreeable with things I do.*

Author: In visiting further with Galen about this dream, we learned his parents drive a Mercedes and his wife's parents drive a Chevrolet. We also learned that the week before this dream, Galen and his wife had hosted a gathering for his wife's family. Galen took care of directing recreation activities for the family while his wife did the cooking for the group.

Although only Galen, the dreamer, could know the meanings of his dream with a certainty, in our view, Galen's dream could be picturing he treats his wife's relatives with great respect -- just as he treats his own relatives with great respect (even those with difficult personalities). Consequently, the "key" that fits his treatment of his family also fits his treatment of his wife's family. Truly beautiful!

Section D

Other Type Dreams, and Putting It All Together

Introduction to Section D

In the first sections of this book, we focused on relationship type dreams. In this Section, we show how the Personalized Method for Interpreting Dreams (PMID) process is easily adapted for working with four other significant categories of dreams:

- **Nightmares**
- **Everyday dreams**
- **Spiritual dreams**
- **Lucid dreams**

In our concluding chapter of Section D, we show you how to put together all you have learned by reviewing past dreams. Reviewing past dreams is essential to refresh dream messages, to help you understand current dreams, to gain new insights, and to correct possible misinterpretations.

As a reminder, we strongly encourage you to record as many of your dreams as you can to (1) acquaint yourself with your own personal dream language, (2) be certain to include dreams that you might not recognize as important at first, and (3) discover dream guidance for all types of activities.

Chapter 11

Facing Nightmares and Scary Dreams, Facing Life

"We either pursue our dreams or our nightmares pursue us."
--Edward Bruce Bynum

The Black Furry Thing

Dream fragment: *A teacher says, "Jane, the black thing," in a warning to me. Before I can move away, something is clamped around my hands as they are clasped (laying) over each other! It is black and furry. I do not open my eyes to look at it; I just feel it. Now it clings to me even tighter! It is so debilitating that it alarms me. It has my hands so tight, I cannot pull them apart and a slight movement makes it tighten its grip. It is not a large "thing"; it may not even be an animal. (It may be more like a very large black caterpillar, but I don't think of that until I write the dream down.) I have awareness I must overcome this although I feel panic-stricken.*

I think how God is all-powerful and can easily rid me of this thing. So after my first reaction of panic, I do pray. I try hard to fight off the panic, but I waken before I can quell the panic and sink into a deep prayer.

Nightmares and other scary dreams can be some of the most traumatic events we face in our lives. Suddenly waking in a sweat-drenched panic following a nightmare is not uncommon, as is the fear that the threat still exists even after waking.

As terrifying as these are, as noted by renowned dream expert Ernest Hartmann, MD, dreams after trauma are the best places to start learning "what is really going on during dreaming . . . because we know exactly what is on the dreamer's mind in an emotionally meaningful sense."[48]

There are three categories of frightening nighttime experiences -- nightmares, night terrors, and the post-traumatic nightmare.[49]

Nightmares are frightening heart-pounding dreams that awaken the dreamer.[50]

"Night terrors are not, strictly speaking, dreams at all."[51] They involve sudden arousal from sleep. Many people experience screaming, profuse sweating, a sense of dread or unreality and often trouble with breathing. "There is little or no imagery associated with the experience, and the person often does not recall it when fully awakened."[52]

Post-traumatic nightmares occur, as the name explains, after the dreamer has experienced serious trauma. Ernest Hartmann,[53] who has made extensive studies of frequent nightmares, says lack of recorded series of dreams following traumatic experiences has acutely hindered research of post-traumatic dreams.

One of our friends found dream help during a time of having post-traumatic nightmares: She asked for comforting dreams. As her post-dream email note confirmed, "Your words of wisdom about asking for comforting dreams worked very well." She dreamed that beloved grandparents came and comforted her -- comforted her so much that she felt no pain and no panic.

If you are one who experiences post-traumatic nightmares, consider asking for comforting dreams. Perhaps ask for someone, human or divine, to come and comfort you.

For those who are having frequent nightmares traceable to some

---

[48] E. Hartmann. *Dreams and Nightmares, The Origin and Meaning of Dreams*. Perseus Publishing, 1998, p. 19.
[49] K. Bulkeley. *An Introduction to the Psychology of Dreaming*. Westport, Conn: Praeger, 1997.
[50] R. Cartwright & L. Lamberg. *Crisis Dreaming, Using Your Dreams to Solve Your Problems*, 1992.
[51] K. Bulkeley. *An Introduction to the Psychology of Dreaming*. Westport, Conn: Praeger, 1997, p. 80.
[52] K. Bulkeley. *An Introduction to the Psychology of Dreaming*. Westport, Conn: Praeger, 1997, p. 80.
[53] E. Hartmann. *Dreams and Nightmares, The Origin and Meaning of Dreams*. Perseus Publishing, 1998.

traumatic event(s) Ernest Hartmann's *Dreams and Nightmares* and Rosalind Cartwright's *Crisis Dreaming,* co-authored with Lynne Lamberg, are the best resources we know of.

Nightmares of being chased or attacked by monsters or strange animals are extremely common among the dreams of three-, four-, and five-year-olds. Although Hartmann has gathered far more adult dreams than children's dreams, his view on children's dreams is:

> I would say that every two- to five-year-old child who is just developing the cognitive structures to realize who is who, who's safe and who's unsafe or unpredictable, and to realize how relatively powerful all the adults are, is bound to have some . . . sense of vulnerability.[54]

Some "early warning" dreams might be considered nightmare type dreams. An example of an early warning dream is one that a dreamer understood cautioned him about accepting an invitation to join a group. Before the dream, the man felt apprehension about the group, but he told himself that he was just being paranoid to resist the group's invitation. In the dream, he is in the room where the meetings are held. As he explores the room, he becomes afraid, decides to get out from there, and even wakes himself out of the dream to avoid the dream situation. He took the cue and got out from the waking situation.

Most people have at least a few nightmares during their lifetimes. Sometimes nightmares stem from what seems like common experiences and they surprise people. A new experience (pleasant or unpleasant) that may seem quite acceptable to us in our waking lives might shock our deeper minds. The stress of being very busy seems like a natural circumstance, but being excessively busy could scare our dreaming minds. Pressing onward rapidly with dreamwork might also scare our dreaming minds.

---

[54] E. Hartmann. *Dreams and Nightmares, The Origin and Meaning of Dreams.* Perseus Publishing, 1998, p. 65.

Do we need to pursue the source of traumatic emotions even after we come to an emotionally comfortable place in our consciousness about them? In our view, the answer is no. Jane, dreamer of "The Black Furry Thing" shown at the opening of this chapter, had other dreams she thought related to the black furry thing. Using those dreams she was successful in overcoming being bothered by her nightmare. Yet she never discovered what the black furry thing represented. Later, she became *"curious what actually happened to bring on that nightmare"* and so decided she was *"brave enough for another dream"* about it. The following nightmare was the result.

Jane's Dream: *Why is it Taking the Man so Long to Die?*

Dream: *I am in a room with other people sitting at tables at a meeting or a class. I prefer to sit on the side of the table, but there doesn't seem to be room there. . . . Oh, well, it is okay to sit at the head of a table, so that is what I do. . . .*

When the meeting/class is over, the rest of the group decides to go someplace else for some relaxing time. I say I cannot go because my mother will be here to pick me up . . . either she or Dad will pick me up. . . . There is something here that I say that isn't quite right. . . . My mother is here and acts like a strict tight-lipped woman superintendent.

The scene changes and I am out front of this place. It is dark. This seems like the Arlington main street. I am standing out in front of a large truck, and I see another truck coming head on. At first I am alarmed for fear the other truck will run into me, but there is a triangle indentation shape in front of both trucks, so that leaves me protected in the inside of this two-triangle place.

The driver, a man, jumps out and quickly goes along a corral here on the street. Oh, my goodness, he has a long barreled gun! He immediately starts firing the gun as he holds it in a horizontal plane and swings it from side to side.

I feel safe from him getting to me physically while I am in this enclosed place. Although I know the bullets could reach me here, I do not feel as concerned that they have as great a chance of hitting me as the other people who would be closer to his range. I do not see any people inside this corral. I am relieved about that.

Oh, my goodness! He quickly lifts the barrel to his mouth and unloads a barrage of pellets, fires them into his tongue. I am beginning to feel terror.

He points the gun at his head and shoots, and shoots, and shoots. His head bleeds and parts of his head blow away, and I think surely he will die soon. I have a relief he has turned the gun on himself and that he will die and I will not need to be afraid of him, but why is it taking so long?

How much damage to his head can he sustain without dying? I wake and think, "This is the worst nightmare I have ever had!"

PMID Step 1: Day-before-dream **event(s)** that connects to this dream.

I am writing an article about abusive behaviors. Last night I asked for a dream about the abuse implied in a nightmare that I titled "The Black Furry Thing" (a black thing covered with fur). Although from working with dreams that came after "The Black-Furry Thing dream" I now feel at ease without knowing details implied by the nightmare, I am curious what actually happened to bring on that nightmare. Yesterday as I sat in our car, I became needlessly concerned about whether a truck backing in would back into our car.

PMID Step 2: Day-before-dream **thought(s)** that connect to this dream.

I debated the wisdom of asking for another dream about the nightmare, but I decided I was brave enough for another dream. I also thought it could be material for my article.

Author: We notice again, the dreamer's thoughts help us go deeper into the reason for the dream. We need only read her thoughts to realize a possible question the dream answered, "Should I ask for another dream about a matter that is now settled?"

PMID Step 3: Major **dream phrases (and symbols)** defined in the context of this dream.

- ***Sit at the head of a table:*** *Decision to be the controller one here and ask for another dream about the source of the nightmare "The Black-Furry Thing".*

- ***Rest of the group decides to go someplace else for some relaxing time:*** *I could have just relaxed about the source of the nightmare. I already feel at ease without knowing details implied by the nightmare, yet I was curious what actually happened to bring on that nightmare.*

- ***Scene changes and I am out front of this place:*** *Place of the setting of the nightmare.*

- ***Is dark:*** *Already shows, Jane, this asking for another dream is way too dark for you to do.*

- ***Standing out in front of a large truck:*** *Connects to an event from the day before this dream when I became needlessly concerned about whether a truck backing in would back into our car. Shows again, Jane you are needlessly asking for the source of the former nightmare.*

- ***Driver, a man, jumps out and quickly goes along a corral here on the street:*** *The nightmare uses the safe driver from the waking life experience to be the nightmare man. Shows again, Jane, you should have stayed in a settled place of mind.*

- ***Immediately starts firing the gun as he holds it in a horizontal plane and swings it from side to side:*** *This is what I, Jane, was doing when I asked for a dream about the source of the former nightmare. I went into a dangerous circumstance.*

- ***Quickly lifts the barrel to his mouth and unloads a barrage of pellets, fires them into his tongue:*** *Another caution—Jane, quiet your words, your tongue. You should not have asked for another dream about this issue.*

- ***Wake and think, "This is the worst nightmare I have ever had!":*** *And this nightmare came when I, Jane, unnecessarily asked for another dream about the issue that had been settled.*

PMID Step 4: Dreaming **emotions** compared with waking life emotions.

My very little concern the truck will run into me during the dream connects to my needless concern yesterday when a truck backed in beside our car. My dream uses that experience to show I am needlessly concerned about what the black furry thing could have represented in my former nightmare.

Terror I feel when the man shoots himself shows I have terrorized myself. Relief when no people are in the corral and relief that he has turned the gun on himself show that I am the only one hurt by my continuing bombardment of my mind.

PMID Step 5: Solutions or suggestions for changing thoughts, attitudes or behaviors (answer[s] to day-before-my-dream thoughts).

In the dream I ask, "Why is it taking so long?" My dream is telling me the issue is over, dead. There would not be any life left in it if I would just let it be. The meeting or class is over. The matter is over. Mother is tight-lipped, caution against doing this.

Author: Curiosity about an alleviated matter can cause alarm -- unnecessary alarm. The dreamer unnecessarily brought the nightmare on herself when she asked for a dream about a matter that no longer bothered her. Notice, the dreamer found the same answer to her pre-dream thoughts in more than one place in the dream!

The next night Jane did close the matter. Read on for her "closing door" dream.

Jane's Dream: *A Door Closes Very Intentionally*

A door is closed. Very intentionally closed with impact. I feel relieved.

PMID Step 1: Day-before-dream **event(s)** that connects to this dream.

I had a nightmare last night after I asked for another dream about the childhood abuse matter.

PMID Step 2: Day-before-dream **thought(s)** that connect to this dream.
After last night's dream, I wondered about the safety of such dreams.

PMID Step 3: Major **dream phrases (and symbols)** defined in the context of this dream.

- ***Door:*** *Door to pursing this particular childhood trauma further.*

PMID Step 4: Dreaming **emotions** compared with waking life emotions.
Relieved in my dream and relieved in waking life.

PMID Step 5: Solutions or suggestions for changing thoughts, attitudes or behaviors (answer[s] to day-before-my-dream thoughts).
Just as in the dream where a door is very intentionally closed with impact, I must deliberately stop thinking about and asking for dreams about a matter that is now dead and over.

Author: For more information about what to look for in your dreams, if you are having nightmares or other scary dreams and need to see someone professionally, please read "A Caveat on Bad or Worrisome Dreams" in our "Considerations for Dreamwork in Clinical Settings," at the end of Section B.

Chapter 12

Everyday Dreams, Everyday Life

Carl Jung once commented about dreamwork "only studying the most dramatic dreams is the same as looking only at the very peak of a mountain and trying to understand the entire mountain range."

Many people make this common mistake as they begin to work with their dreams. In their search for life-changing insights, they frequently overlook the more mundane dreams and miss a wealth of valuable knowledge about themselves and their world. Again, dreams mirror our waking lives in which the vast majority of our experiences are rather common, yet no less important.

Our more common everyday dreams are also important for learning our dream language and preparing us for those that are more dramatic. These give us perspectives, understanding, and holistic views just like our everyday life provides the basis for our understanding of significant events.

We focus on these everyday life dreams in this chapter. **For our purposes in this book, we define an everyday dream as any dream that focuses on common activities such as work, recreation, career, education, health, and the spiritual. For the purposes of this book, we define relationship dreams as dreams about our reactions to others.** Of course, everyday dream types and relationship dream types can overlap.

A dream journal[55] published this first dream, interpretations, and comments with slight modifications in the early 1990's.

---

[55] E. Duesbury. "Professor Uses Dreams as Guides in Working with Students," *Dream Network*, *13*(2).

Don't Ask Your Students to Wash Their Dirty Laundry in Public

Background: *In my work as an associate professor, I am catching fascinating glimpses of an ever-present Counselor who has finally caught my attention by speaking to me in my dreams. Imagine my delight at discovering my theater of the night also acts as a light by day as I teach students.*

Dream: *People are washing clothes in a laundry area of our apartment building. They brought the clothes up from the basement. I bring my clothes to wash also. A woman who was washing in the basement is now washing upstairs in this public laundry sort of area. A young man, probably a college student, is standing close to her and when he sees me, he says very loudly and possessively to me, "I'm next."*

I take my basket of clothes downstairs and talk loudly in mimic of the young man's "I'm next" as I go down the stairs. However, when I arrive in the basement, I understand why these people aren't washing in the basement. Either there aren't machines here now, or they aren't working. The upstairs is more like a public laundry than the basement.

PMID Step 1: Day-before-dream **event(s)** that connects to this dream.

I assigned an ethics case to my business students. The case involved a graduating senior who had job interviews at two separate companies in the same city. Upon discovering he would be reimbursed for interviewing expenses, the student billed both companies for the full amount of his expenses.

In our brief class discussion, a couple of students openly said they would have done the same thing; that is, take double reimbursement; it would help on college expenses. Some other students said they would not have taken the double reimbursement; it did not seem ethical to them. I reminded my students that it is needful to be considerate of all people involved in circumstances.

Later, when I read the students' written responses to the ethics question, I was surprised to find that several students said they would have taken the double reimbursement.

PMID Step 2: Day-before-dream **thought(s)** that connect to this dream.

I decided to talk about the case in class again. I gave considerable thought to how I would approach the matter without inhibiting the students from feeling free to express themselves openly and honestly in class. In early morning the day I planned to give my "little talk," the above dream came.

Author: Now the plot gets thicker as we realize the professor's thoughts pose a question for the dream to answer, perhaps "Will the students respond well to my talk?"

PMID Step 3: Major **dream phrases (and symbols)** defined in the context of this dream.

- ***Clothes:*** *Often symbolic of the personality.*

- ***Are washing clothes in a laundry area of our apartment building:*** *In the topic of this dream the people who are washing clothes are students in my business class. At the time of this dream, we are living in an apartment building. The laundry area is downstairs from where our apartment is located. Basement, in the topic of this dream, symbolizes the privacy area.*

- ***Brought the clothes up from the basement:*** *In the topic of this dream, if I decide to bring up the ethics case in class again, symbolically I would be asking my students to leave their privacy area, and openly discuss their written responses to the ethics case assignment.*

- ***Bring my clothes to wash also:*** *Would the decision to talk about the ethics case in class again reflect "unwashed" considerations on my part?*

- ***Woman who was washing in the basement is now washing upstairs in this public laundry sort of area:*** *Possible reactions by students who wrote intuitive knowing answers to the ethics case if I discuss the ethics case in class again. I am one who goes with the concept that unidentified female responses in both male and female dreams have potential to symbolize intuitive knowing.*

- ***Young man, probably a college student, is standing close to her and when he sees me, he says very loudly and possessively to me, "I'm next":*** *Possible logical reasoning reactions by students who wrote their logical reasoning answers to the ethics case if I discuss the ethics case in class again. I am one who goes with the concept that unidentified male responses in both male and female dreams have potential to symbolize logical reasoning.*

- ***Take my basket of clothes downstairs and talk loudly in mimic of the young man's "I'm next" as I go down the stairs:*** *In the event I discuss the students' written responses to the ethics question in class, it will be a mimic of the students who wrote logical reasoning responses to the ethics question assignment.*

- ***As I go down the stairs:*** *As I think intuitively about the possibility to discuss the students' written responses to the ethics question in class.*

- ***When I arrive in the basement, I understand why these people aren't washing in the basement:*** *In my intuitive knowing I do understand why it would be unwise to discuss the ethics question again in class.*

- ***Either there aren't machines here now, or they aren't working:*** *This scene symbolizes the circumstance in the event I decide to talk again about the students' reactions to the ethics case. That decision will leave the students with no choice but to discuss in the public of our classroom what they should be allowed to contemplate in the sanctuary of their private minds.*

- ***Upstairs is more like a public laundry than the basement:*** *This means the public that our classroom is. It is a public area in contrast to the students being allowed to contemplate the ethics case in the sanctuary of their inner selves.*

Author: Again we see that universal meanings expanded by the dreamer's personal experiences make sense of the dream symbols. Clothes and levels of a building are universal symbols.

PMID Step 4: Dreaming **emotions** compared with waking life emotions.

My dreaming emotion, by implication, is surprise at there being no washing machines in the basement. Before this dream, though I had given the matter considerable thought, I still did not feel completely at ease with what I planned to say.

PMID Step 5: Solutions or suggestions for changing thoughts, attitudes or behaviors (answer[s] to day-before-my-dream thoughts).

The dream answers my day-before-the-dream thoughts by showing that my planned talk about the students' written responses to the ethics case is like asking my students to "wash their dirty laundry in public." That is, if I decide to talk about the students' written reactions to the ethics case in class, I will be asking my students to discuss in the public of our classroom what they should be allowed to contemplate in the sanctuary of their private minds.

How I Used My Dream: *When I went to class, I gave each student a copy of the textbook authors' comments on the ethics case. I also made a note to myself to assign the ethics cases from most of the chapters we will cover. I did not give my planned little talk.*

Author: The next two dreams deal with another area of everyday life--how to keep from feeling overwhelmed with workloads.

Shawn's Dream: *Something Moves My House over My Pool*

Dream: *I am at some unknown house. It is raining very hard. There is lots of water. At some time, I am back at my own house. My house is sort of unfamiliar. It is raining here, too. I don't seem to be particularly concerned, except I wonder about all the rain. The water is not turbulent.*

My house starts to move. It is moved back over my pool as I sit inside. And then my house settles in here over the pool. I have the feeling of, "Well, here I am. I will deal with this."

PMID Step 1: Day-before-dream **event(s)** that connects to this dream.
My colleagues and I are swamped with work.

Author: We can connect the rain in the dream with Shawn's waking life "swamp" of work to understand his dream theme--*overcome with work demands.*

PMID Step 2: Day-before-dream **thought(s)** that connect to this dream.
Last night I thought about the mounting workload and wondered how we are ever going to get all this swamp of work done.

PMID Step 3: Major **dream phrases (and symbols)** defined in the context of this dream.

- **Raining very hard:** *"It never rains but it pours" workload for my colleagues and me now. The workload keeps mounting; we don't know how long the flooding of work will keep up.*

- **Pool:** *A quiet body of water, a refreshing restful place.*

- **My house moved with me inside:** *Connection between my home life and me.*

- **House settling in over my pool:** *I am being moved to a quiet, refreshing place.*

PMID Step 4: Dreaming **emotions** compared with waking life emotions.
In my dream, I am not particularly concerned about all the rain, although in waking life I feel a lot of pressure from the mounting workload. In the dream, the water is not turbulent. In waking life, my work situation looks to be very turbulent.

Author: We are surprised to see the contrasts between dreamer's "not particularly concerned" emotions and "not turbulent" water in the dream and the waking life pressure he felt from the mounting workload.

PMID Step 5: Solutions or suggestions for changing thoughts, attitudes or behaviors (answer[s] to day-before-my-dream thoughts).

My dream shows to have some "Shawn time" at home to keep from feeling flooded at work. Move myself into a quiet emotional calm.

Ruth's Dream: *I and My Little Scoop Shovel*

I am in my vehicle. It isn't a car. It is perhaps an open four-wheeler of some kind. It is parked with cars around a circle drive at a public place, perhaps a schoolhouse.

A lot of snow has fallen around the cars and the circle drive. Some people drive their cars out and leave tracks as they go. Although I can now drive my vehicle through, I nevertheless get out and dig some of the deep tracks on the side.

I look and see a big blue semi-truck coming. It has a snow scraper on front, and I know it will very easily scrape the snow away. But I still scoop a bit with my little shovel. I don't scoop snow laboriously, though, really to be moving the snow; I scoop so the truck driver sees I am scooping!

PMID Step 1: Day-before-dream **event(s)** that connects to this dream.

Last night I affirmed that my work this upcoming semester would be easily manageable.

Author: To arrive at the dream's theme, the dreamer simply connects the "snowed-in" circumstances of waking life work with the "snowed-in" vehicle in the dream, to arrive at the theme -- *difficulty with managing my workload.*

PMID Step 2: Day-before-dream **thought(s)** that connect to this dream.

Last night I wondered how I could manage my workload to have less stress.

- 137 -

Author: Okay, we see how connecting this pre-dream thought to the dream builds on the theme developed in the dreamer's Step 1 connection as if to ask the question, *"How can I manage my workload so I am less stressed?"*

PMID Step 3: Major **dream phrases (and symbols)** defined in the context of this dream.

- ***Open four-wheeler of some kind:*** *In the context of this dream represents my physical body, the "vehicle" that transports me.*

- ***Lot of snow has fallen around the cars:*** *My snowed-in feeling from my work.*

- ***Circle drive:*** *Going in circles. (There is no circle drive at the school where I work.)*

- ***People drive their cars out and leave tracks as they go:*** *Colleagues who have gone before me have left directions for accomplishing some of the tasks I do. I can easily follow their tracks, their guidances.*

- ***Big blue truck coming with a blade:*** *Help far in excess of mental chugging away. The truck's color, blue, represents "Spiritual."*[56] *For this dream, the intuitive-spiritual power of my mind.*

- ***Still scoop a bit with my little shovel:*** *Unnecessary work.*

- ***Scoop so the truck driver sees I am scooping:*** *I do unnecessary work just to be recognized.*

Author: Notice the helpfulness these symbol phrase definitions are in continuing to build toward a solution to the dreamer's dilemma. Notice, too, that the dream is "telling on" Ruth when it reveals she does

---

[56] J. Boushahla and V. Reidel-Geubtner. *The Dream Dictionary*. NY: Berkley Books, 1992.

unnecessary work just to be recognized. Ruth accepts this from her dream; would she be so quick to accept this from another person?

PMID Step 4: Dreaming **emotions** compared with waking life emotions.

I did not record my dreaming emotions. My unnecessary scooping shows my desire to impress others overshadows the help I could receive. In waking life, I feel strained from all the work of the upcoming semester.

PMID Step 5: Solutions or suggestions for changing thoughts, attitudes or behaviors (answer[s] to day-before-my-dream thoughts).

Stop doing unnecessary work just to impress others.

There are three opportunities for me to avoid becoming snowed in and having to dig myself out. First, I am a very strong and energetic person and I have plenty of stamina to pull me through demanding work schedules. I have already equipped myself with fine lectures and supplementary materials. However, I do extra work that is unnecessary, as it is unnecessary to scoop snow in front of a four-wheel drive vehicle.

Second, others have gone before me and I can easily follow their tracks. I can use, for example, textbook authors' supplementary materials instead of generating new materials.

Third, there is a big blue truck coming with a blade. When I think from a high point of positive consciousness, creative ideas flow naturally.

How I Use My Dream: *I work consciously to stand back in a listening attitude as the "Big Blue Truck" does the work. It is hard work to stand back and listen, but if I'm ever going to handle the work I must listen to wisdom that is beyond my foolish pride.*

Author: Hank's ability to listen to his "intuitively derived" messages in the next dream helped him avoid possible excessive financial demands.

Hank's Dream: *Rain, Mud, and Added Farm Costs*

Dream: *This was a quite a dream. I was back home, not living there, must have been shortly after I graduated from college and was back home. Dad and I went* *out into the feed and barn lots where I helped Dad with some type of fussing work. The feedlots and barn lots were very muddy, deep mud. It had been raining a lot.*

Then the mail carrier came. He seemed almost familiar to me, but I don't recall now who he was. For some reason he came up and visited with Dad and me.

Then shortly a woman and her three very active kids stopped by. I didn't know her. The kids must have been somewhere between four years old and eight years old because they were very active in playing in the mud. While we were out there, it started raining again so we had to go to the house to get out of the rain.

When I got to the door I could see there was mud all over the floors, thick mud, several inches deep, on the floor and the furniture from the kids coming in with mud, and, of course, some manure, manure from the feedlots. Dad was behind me. I turned around and said to him, warned him what he would see in the house. "Before you come in, just realize that Mom is going to need all new furniture to replace the furniture in here. Just know that, and factor the cost of the new furniture into the farm costs."

PMID Step 1: Day-before-dream **event(s)** that connects to this dream.

Yesterday I made a follow-up appointment with a real estate agent who wants to sell a small farm to me. The farm is near my parents' land. I'd like to have it for my pleasure; it isn't a need.

PMID Step 2: Day-before-dream **thought(s)** that connect to this dream.

I thought about the asking price and about a counter offer approach.

Author: We see Hank's thought connections take us to a thought question the dream might "answer," *How much should I offer for the farm?*

PMID Step 3: Major **dream phrases (and symbols)** defined in the context of this dream.

- ***Feedlots and barn lots were very muddy:*** *Lots of water from adjoining farms flows over the farm I am thinking of buying.*

- ***Deep mud:*** *Mud can sink into old tile from heavy rain and plug the tile.*

- ***For some reason he [mail carrier] came up and visited with Dad and me:*** *A message for us in the dream.*

- ***Kids . . . playing in the mud:*** *I want the land for my pleasure. I don't need it.*

- ***[In the house could see] some manure, manure from the feedlots:*** *The current price of the land is a "shitty deal."*

- ***Going to need all new furniture to replace the furniture in here:*** *The water flowing over the for-sale land will result in later costs to replace existing water drainage systems.*

PMID Step 4: Dreaming **emotions** compared with waking life emotions.

Pretty disturbed in my dream. I have been amazed at the amount of water flowing through the farm, but I have been unconcerned since I see no evidence of need to replace existing water draining devices.

Author: Again, we see a difference between dreaming emotions and waking life emotions about a circumstance. And this isn't even a relationship dream! Emotions connect in so much of life, not only interactions with others.

PMID Step 5: Solutions or suggestions for changing thoughts, attitudes or behaviors (answer[s] to day-before-my-dream thoughts).

A thought question the dream might "answer," *How much should I offer for the farm?* The dreamer's answer is:

Telling Dad to factor the cost of the furniture into farm costs advises me I need to factor cost of new water drainage systems into my offer to buy, if I do offer to buy the farm.

Author: Look closer at the settings of these everyday dreams -- a public laundry, a pool, a circle drive, and a muddy farm. Quite common settings. Now look at the dreamers' interpretations of those common-setting dreams. The public laundry prevented a talk from alienating a classroom of students, the pool gave a man a way out of feeling overwhelmed about work, the circle drive helped a busy professor use "wisdom beyond my foolish pride," and the muddy farm dream likely saved the farmer dreamer thousands of dollars.

What valuable tools dreams are!

You ask, "Why didn't these people think of these solutions in waking life?" We wonder, too. Perhaps they did think of them, yet neglected to act until the dreamers' intuitively derived interpretations prodded their confidence that these were the best solutions.

More likely, they had thought of only part of the solutions contained in each dream and the dreams tossed in some "added wisdom." Dreams are very good at tossing in added wisdom that we have not considered in waking life.

Watch your dreams to see if this is true for you. Instead of saying of a dream, "Oh, that dream is just regurgitation of what I did yesterday," say, "I wonder what added wisdom my dream is telling me about what I did yesterday."

Chapter 13

Spiritual Dreams, Spiritual Life

"Dreams have been regarded as a valuable source of spiritual insight, inspiration, and guidance by virtually every cultural and religious tradition in the world."[57] "The current resurgence of interest in and use of dreamwork for the age-old purpose of spiritual growth and development is most hopeful and offers both challenges and possibilities innate within the dream."[58]

We borrow from Bulkeley to define what we mean in this book by the term, spiritual dreams: "Those dreams that bring people experientially closer to the powers of the sacred and that speak to their ultimate existential concerns. . . . Such dreams are experienced by both 'religious' people and 'secular' people alike."[59]

> *I am overcome with the Force that surrounds me and moves around my body -- and moves me* [what I have felt on occasion in waking state — but this is a dream]. *I feel afraid. I scream but now I realize it is okay and I drop my resistance. Instantly, or immediately, or as soon as I drop my resistance to the Moving around my body, very intense, I am aware for a fleeting moment that Jesus is with me. I don't see Him; I just know for that magnificent instant He is here.*
> ~ Undisclosed dreamer

What constitutes a numinous or spiritual dream for you? Must a divine figure come? Or as a "knowing" instead of a conceived "figure"?

---

[57] K. Bulkeley. *Spiritual Dreaming, a Cross-cultural and Historical Journey*. Paulist Press, 1992, p. 2.
[58] B. Wollmering. "Dreams and Spirituality: An Historical Perspective," *Dream Time*, a Publication of the Association for the Study of Dreams, 1997.
[59] K. Bulkeley. *Spiritual Dreaming, a Cross-cultural and Historical Journey*. Paulist Press, 1992, p. 3.

Or a voice or a light? Or could dreams devoid of deity figures, felt presences, voices, or lights, qualify as helpful for spiritual growth?

Would you, as Bulkeley[60] claims, consider the following dream topics sacred: The dead, snakes, nightmares, sexuality, and flying?

These symbols, of course, have various type meanings. Take the snake, for example. Have you had snake dreams where you understand a snake as objectively symbolized? For instance one night after speaking unkindly to my husband, a baseball player, I dreamed a snake named "Mr. K" struck out at me. When I told my dream to my husband, he explained "K" in baseball records means "strikeout."

Have you had snake dreams that seem to have a numinous quality? For instance, one night after reading an article by Eric Butterworth[61] I dreamed a man offered a snake to me. In the context of that dream, I understood the snake had a spiritual meaning.

Spiritual-type dreams are often interrelated with relationship-type dreams. This interrelatedness coupled with the powerful reality that dreams make "connections more widely, more broadly than waking (thoughts)"[62] makes dream interpretation an extremely valuable tool for understanding ourselves. Look for whether that is true in any of the dreams in this chapter.

Note: All dreamers' words (Background, Dream and PMID steps) are in italics.

This next dreamer may seem like a personal counselor of some kind. She was not.

Beth's Dream: *God Speaks to Me*

I am down in the basement of our new house with others, including my husband and a son. I tell little boy Nathan, when he wakes in the morning the first thing is we

---

[60] K. Bulkeley. *Spiritual Dreaming, a Cross-cultural and Historical Journey.* Paulist Press. 1992.
[61] Butterworth, Eric. "The School of Life," *Centerpeace.* Vol. 11 - No. 1. New York: The Unity Center of New York, September/October 1996.
[62] E. Hartmann. *Dreams and Nightmares, The Origin and Meaning of Dreams.* Perseus Publishing, 1998, p. 11.

will give him a bath. Bath doesn't get taken and I make further efforts to get the bath done. Goeff tells me to let Nathan decide for himself on the bath. I tell Goeff I am right in going ahead with Nathan's bath.

Going up to the main floor from the basement, there is a very small hole, like a large mail slot, and seems to have some kind of padding around it (felt strip?) to drop down through to go to the main floor. Seems quite inconvenient and seems people like Mom couldn't do this because of the small slot.

Upstairs on the main floor I marvel at the cement walls. No decoration on them. I think that unusual for anyone. We are satisfied with them with only the plain cement. In some places mortar has run down making some mars on the wall. I think probably will effect marketability of our house without wall coverings.

Main floor is a long room. The room is empty.

I now realize <u>I am dreaming</u>.

I hear God's voice. I am aware the room is full of a golden light. This is delicious!

I do a few running steps. What shall I do now that I know I am dreaming? Know not to do any "tricks," but to "just be."

I say, "I love you, God," and a voice comes back, "<u>I love you</u>." No recall whether God says my name.

God continues to talk as I listen. But there is interference. God's voice seems so far away, I can hardly hear Him. How surprising God "can't" or "doesn't" speak so I can hear Him clearly. Feel to ask Him to speak louder. I do hear Him say through the interference that it is other things I have on my mind that make "static" and drowns out hearing God.

Other people are in the room. I think to put my attention fully on God and get back to hearing Him. There are some young girls and one has a disability of some kind. Others don't seem to want my attention, but this one lays on me as I push or walk her around. I'll do this and then get back to listening to God.

The activity in the room increases. There is a broken off piece of needle-like or pin in my leg. As I go to pull it out, I see a young man who has several pieces of this broken off metal needle-width pieces in his legs. I help him pull them out. He is in pain. (Mine didn't seem to hurt me, although I continue to think how I'll get back to mine and pull the one out I know about.)

There is a medical person who is pulling some of these "pins" out of this boy's neck. I hold the boy around the upper back to comfort him and help ease the pain as these needles are being pulled out.

Step 1: Day-before-dream **event(s)** that connects to this dream.

Some time ago I gave up listening to tapes for my meditation time. The past several nights I have had trouble getting to sleep. So last night, I listened to a meditation tape that features Light. Last night during that tape, for the first time, when I made more conscious effort than before in "being the Light," I had a sense of the Light. I fell asleep with the tape and dreamed this dream.

Yesterday I started work on connecting thought with light, something I have tried to do before. From those events, the theme of this dream must be meditation.

Step 2: Day-before-dream **thought(s)** that connect to this dream.

Last night, I finally thought I do need some outside help, and the thought came to listen to the "Light" meditation tape again.

Step 3: Major **dream phrases (and symbols)** defined in the context of this dream.

- ***Down in the basement of our new house with others, including my husband and a son:*** *Something new here was I listened to the "Light" meditation tape again. I hadn't listened to the tape in a long time. New could also mean, a new level of meditation from when I have meditated before.*

- ***Tell little boy Nathan, when he wakes in the morning the first thing is we will give him a bath:*** *These actions connect, likely to my waking life giving unneeded suggestions to one of our grown sons. Bath is symbolic of cleansing.*

- ***Goeff tells me to let Nathan decide for himself on the bath:*** *True. In looking back, sure I know that is true.*

- ***Tell Goeff I am right in going ahead with Nathan's bath:*** *Goodnight! I wasn't right. Good my dream told me.*

- ***Up to the main floor from the basement, there is a very small hole, like a large mail slot, and seems to have some kind of***

- ***padding around it (felt strip?):*** *In going into meditation, emotions (feelings, the felt strip), need to be quieted.*

- **Drop down through to go to the main floor:** *During the meditation about Light, the person is guided down into the center of his or her being.*

- **Seems people like Mom couldn't do this because of the small slot:** *Don't know except could the weight symbolize "heavy issues" for my mom to work through? Or, more likely, do heavy issues about my mom mean issues I need to work through?*

- **Down in the basement of our new house:** *Inside of the house means mind sometimes. Something new is the more intense push I am making for divine contact.*

- **Now realize <u>I am dreaming</u>:** *So could have asked some questions or done other activities. Didn't though.*

- **Hear God's voice:** *I sincerely believe I "heard" some form of divine presence during my dream.*

- **Aware the room is full of a golden light:** *Divine Presence. This scene signifies ties I made to light and thought. Also comes from listening to the meditation tape.*

- **What shall I do now that I know I am dreaming ... Know not to do any "tricks," but to "just be":** *Exactly, when in lucid dream states, for me anyway, know not to do any tricks, but to "just be".*

- **Say, "I love you, God," and a voice comes back, "<u>I love you</u>":** *Oh, so, so beyond comprehension, and so, so, meaningful. Success filled meditation.*

- **Hear Him say through the interference that it is other things I have on my mind that make "static" and drowns out**

- ***hearing God:*** *This is what happened next in the dream...my wandering thoughts drowned out my feelings of the Presence.*

- **Think to put my attention fully on God and get back to hearing Him:** *My intentions are to put my full attention on meditational feeling the Presence. Though, as the rest of the dream shows, my attention to waking life issues catapulted me out of meditation.*

- **Some young girls and one has a disability of some kind . . . lays on me as I push or walk her around:** *A person becoming dependent on me, which I allowed. Something I don't want for her sake, and not for my sake.*

- **I'll do this and then get back to listening to God:** *Again intentions to return to deep meditations.*

- **Piece of needle-like or pin in my leg:** *I, too, have pains, symbolic, issues I need to pull from my legs (my understanding). Legs symbolize understanding.*

- **Young man who has several pieces of this broken off metal needle-width pieces in his legs:** *Symbol of pins in the body originated some time ago when I read a pastor's dream about a person he was helping. Again leges symbolize (my understanding). Some understandings are inhibiting this young man's ability to do such as meditation.*

- **Help him pull them out:** *Ties to my tryings to help a young man pull out—overcome some hurtful issues in his life.*

- **Medical person who is pulling some of these "pins" out of this boy's neck . . . I hold the boy around the upper back to comfort him and help ease the pain as these needles are being pulled out:** *The medical person is a professional person. Could be there was real medical issues in this young man's body. My attempt to help maybe did ease his pain, whatever it really was. Nevertheless, I needed to have overcome some stressful issues in my life before I would have been able to fully* *help "ease" whatever pain this young man was having.*

Step 4: Dreaming and waking life **emotions** compared about dream issue or relationship.

My dreaming emotions expressed as "oh, this is delicious," shows my absolute delight in hearing God. I didn't record my pre-dream waking life emotions at the time of this dream about if I could hear God.

Step 5: Solutions or suggestions for changing thoughts, attitudes or behaviors (answer[s] to day-before-my-dream thoughts)

In answer to my last night's thoughts about needing some help to quiet myself in meditation, keep from interfering with Nathan's "cleansing" work, work through restrictive emotions that may linger from my experiences with my mom, avoid letting others become dependent on me, and rid myself of limited understanding before I try to help others.

Success in making these changes will quiet me for meditation because then my thoughts about my helping efforts will no longer be so active they crowd out "hearing God"—divine intuitive messages. A humbling message.

Step 6: Main **relationship** plus dreaming and waking life **reactions** to each person in dream.

Main relationships are my family and people who I try to help. My reaction to my husband is to ignore his sage advice. I do that sometimes when I am awake, too. My reaction to our youngest son, (a grown person), is to treat him like a very young child. I do that sometimes when I am awake, too. In my dream and awake my reaction to people I see in pain is to try to help them. In the process much of the time my mind becomes too occupied to be conscious of Divine Presence; and I become a pain instead of a help.

The good news is I seem to be capable of taking care of my own hurts without pain, at least was when I started to pull the pin out of my leg in this dream. If and when I succeed to interact with others without activating interfering emotional thoughts, will I be more capable of "hearing" God, Divine Presence, higher thoughts at times?

Author: Though the dreamer may seem like a personal counselor of some kind, as we said, she was not. People in all walks of life can use dreams to reveal when "lending a hand" to others is beneficial and when not. And all can use dreams to understand what thoughts, attitudes (emotions), and behaviors would be more helpful to others and self if changed. Notice benefits of a clear mind.

Lawrence's Dream: *Fire and Water and Dad at the Family Gathering*

I am at a park at a family gathering when Dad and I leave and walk down a path through the woods to some type body of water. It may be a lake or it may be just a pond. After we arrive at the lake-pond, we notice there is a fire in the bushes nearby. As we look back down the path, we see many fires along the way we just came.

We become alarmed and hurry to go back down the path to the park and the family gathering. We fight fires the whole way back to the park.

Author: The man who dreamed the above dream offered no interpretations of his dream, though he expressed awe at his dream; so we are unsure whether he views the archetypes in his dream (fire and water) as numinous symbols.

We do notice his dream includes relationships. The dream seems to connote resistance to being away from the family. When danger occurs, the dreamer and his dad hurry back to the family gathering. In contrast, the dreamer of "Resistance to Leaving the Balcony," shown next, resists to stop at the parents' drive.

Karin's Dream: *Resistance to Leaving the Balcony*

I am at a place with a large round balcony that looks out into the sky. My husband is here. I want to stay longer, but cannot explain why. It seems if I stay, it will just be more of looking into the sky (because that is all that I have experienced). We leave.

We are walking. Our youngest son is with us. He doesn't look like himself, though. He is more stoutly built and not as light and cheerful as he was when he was a young child. But he is a young child. . . .

Later we are riding on a bicycle. I am on the back. My husband is peddling and steering. Though I do not see our son, I know my husband put him on this bicycle in front of him.

It is a bit scary for me because we are going fast, and I cannot see where we are going. I think of the danger of falling, but I also think about how my husband has good balance.

We come to my parents' place. I want to continue the journey, but again I cannot think of a solid logical reason to do so.

PMID Step 1: Day-before-dream **event(s)** that connects to this dream.

I set aside special times this weekend for long meditations. Thus, the theme of this dream is meditations.

PMID Step 2: Day-before-dream **thought(s)** that connect to this dream.

Last night I thought how easily I sink into a quiet state and remain for long periods during meditation. Thus, a likely thought-question to which this dream may respond is: Are my current meditation abilities progressing me onward in spiritual expansion?

PMID Step 3: Major **dream phrases (and symbols)** defined in the context of this dream.

- ***Balcony that looks out into the sky:*** *Hope for spiritual expansion, higher consciousness.*

- ***Want to stay longer:*** *Obviously when I can "easily I sink into a quiet state and remain for long periods during meditation" I desire continuance of those results.*

- ***Cannot explain why:*** *My dream lets me know though I want to continue the level of these meditations, there is no reason to continue at this level, given my aspirations for spiritual expansion.*

- ***Just be more of looking into the sky:*** *Stalemate in my spiritual progress, in higher consciousness.*

- ***Youngest son is with us . . . doesn't look like himself:*** *Way I currently see this son is inaccurate.*

- ***Are riding on a bicycle:*** *Our need to individualize from each other in terms of working toward emotional maturity. The scene is reminiscent of times we constrained the rules and capacity of a small motorcycle and all three of us rode on the same small cycle.*

- ***Husband is peddling and steering:*** *Though I do have confidence in his stability, the idea of only following my husband's "driving," his lead, instead of doing some contemplation for myself limits both of our progress.*

- ***Bit scary for me because we are going fast, and I cannot see where we are going:*** *When I refrain from thinking for myself, it leaves no opportunities for me to expand my consciousness.*

- ***My parents' place:*** *I need to explore my relationships with my parents.*

- ***Want to continue the journey, but again I cannot think of a solid logical reason to do so:*** *Resistance to exploring parental relationships. There is no reason to pass by these issues without dealing with them.*

PMID Step 4: Dreaming **emotions** compared with waking life emotions.

My dreaming emotions are resistance to leaving exclusive concentration on spiritual pursuits and resistance to exploring relationships with my family of origin and nuclear family. My waking life emotions about exploring relationships with my family are that I realize I still have uncomfortable feelings about some of those relationships, but I have not thought of those as impeding my spiritual pursuits.

Author: Dreaming emotions tell a great deal about the dreamer that dreamers might hesitate to accept or even be aware of from thinking about in waking states.

PMID Step 5: Solutions or suggestions for changing thoughts, attitudes or behaviors (answer[s] to day-before-my-dream thoughts).
My dream counsels me to attend to unresolved emotional issues about my experiences with my family of origin and my nuclear family before I am ready to spend all my time "on the balcony" of higher consciousness.

Author: Know yourself echoes through innumerable theologies. We view this dream as a classical dream that encourages the dreamer to understand reactions in relationship experiences during pursuits of spiritual awareness.

PMID Step 6: Dreaming and waking life **reactions** to each person in this dream.
This dream seems to show that some youthful experiences influence my interactions with my husband and our children. In retrospect, though I did understand that the dream shows I needed to work through unresolved relationship issues about my family, I had no realization at the time of the dream that dreamwork would be a major avenue for alleviating stress from earlier relationship experiences. Actually, I had no realization as to the depth that unresolved relationship matters affected me at the time of this dream.

Author: Notice the generational systems effects in the above dream: The dream depicts three generations. As we take notice of effects that previous generation experiences have on our current relationship experiences -- healthy and unhealthy -- we catch glimpses of possible effects on generations that succeed us.

We suggest that you review the "Fire and Water" dream (dream before this one) and "Resistance to Leaving the Balcony" (above). Decide whether you believe either is only about relationships or is only about the spiritual, or if both interconnect relationships with spirituality.

Deep water concerns when working with spiritual dreams

At the beginning of one of the dream interpretation courses that I (author, Evelyn M. Duesbury) taught, consultant-to-me Edward Bruce Bynum and I agreed spiritual dreamwork would best be left out of the course. However, students mentioned spirituality on their applications, so we waited for students to bring the topic up on the discussion board.

However, before the topic came up, I gave in to a strong intuition and sent the following email to a student in response to a statement on the student's application:

> One frustration you state is "my lack of connection to spirituality." . . . When I feel frustrated about such things, I sometimes help myself by recalling a favorite teacher's words, "God, spirit, loves a questioning mind." Another (Edward Bruce Bynum) says, "Spirit breathes through dreams if we will breath in spirit during our waking hours." Perhaps these will help.

At about the time I sent the email, the student put an item on the discussion board about spiritual dreaming. That night I had the following dream:

Spiritual Dreaming -- *Where to Swim -- and Where to take Caution*

There is large pond of water. There are some -- seems like some of my students along a high cliff's edge where there are rocks under the water below and looks like long "un-swum" waters. The water here looks ancient and the round rocks seem to have settlings on them.

The students who are over here are so close to the edge I am fearful they will fall in or perhaps even voluntarily jump. There is a "swimming part" up farther where people are swimming and that is okay to go in there.

The students who are here are from this local area and I think they likely would have been in this part of the pond when they were younger. But, I feel a caution now that they will get near the edge and a caution about whether they should go in here where there are rocks and it is sort of deep.

How I Used My Dream: I put the following post on the class discussion board:

Spiritual dreamwork reminds me of a large lake that has a couple of places that might invite us to swim. One place in the lake is a safe place to swim -- the water is clear. Another place in the lake has a high cliff overlooking the water below, and as we stand and look below, we have the feeling that this is an ancient spot. Although we may have faint recall of having been in this part of the lake when we were children, the lake looks foreboding here now. The water is murky and there are settlings on the rocks just under the water that make us think that few if any people have been in the water here recently.

We could jump in here; and it is often tempting to do so. Yet, we do not know what is under the surface of the water. . . . Writers are quick to say that people on spiritual quests (either consciously or unconsciously) are confronted with relationship dreams. . . .

In my view, all dreams are helpful dreams though sometimes they may not seem that way. We do need to be cautious where we swim. Do not go swimming alone when the lake looks foreboding.

Chapter 14

Lucid Dreams, Living Dreams

> The fully lucid dreams . . . are instances of transcendental experiences, experiences in which you go beyond your current level of consciousness. Lucid dreamers (at least during the dream) have gone beyond their former views of themselves and have entered a higher state of consciousness.
> --S. LaBerge, *Lucid Dreaming: The Power of Being Awake and Aware in Your Dreams*

It is a scientific fact that during lucid dreaming, the dreamer is aware of being in a dream and to some extent can control the dream content. Stephen LaBerge is one who has studied lucid dreaming extensively. He considers lucid dreaming valuable for recreational and psychological applications, as well as for scientific study of dreaming and REM sleep.

However, some dream authorities reject the idea of manipulating dreams. For them, during non-lucid dreaming, the Cognitive Sensor is locked away from bowdlerizing the dreaming mind's exploration into the vast, vast territories of the psyche's rich accumulations. So, why on earth would anyone want to let the Cognitive Sensor in to manipulate his or her dreams?

> Some people may decide that ordinary dreams bring so much enjoyment and understanding that lucid dreams add little if anything to their wisdom and appreciation. . . . Others may find that lucid dreaming is an altered state of consciousness that brings excitement, delight, and knowledge that can be obtained in no other way. Some dreamers claim to have held conversations with God in their lucid dreams, while others report that their lucid dreams are more constricted and less creative than their ordinary dreams. . . . Each

person must decide for him or herself whether lucid dreaming is worth the effort.[63]

We agree with Krippner and Dillard that "lucid dreaming is not for everyone," but "the knowledge that such a phenomenon is possible, and has been demonstrated in the sleep laboratory, should encourage individuals who have chosen this way to facilitate creative problem-solving in their dreams."[64]

Author: Read the following dream and you not only will have an excellent definition of what lucid dreaming is you will also have some hints for retaining lucidity during dreaming.

Noah's Dream: *Lucid Dream -- Teach Others How to Fly*

Last night I had a dream in which I was high up in the air and an object came floating by. Immediately I noticed this, realized the oddness and flying motif, and, thus, deduced that I must be dreaming.
Quickly, I told myself to remain calm and, therein, maintain the state of lucidity. This I did and several other events in the dreamwork unfolded. However, I did not lose lucidity and eventually people I knew were in the landscape.
At first, I was the only person in the situation who could consciously and willfully fly. I offered to help the three or four others, one of whom was my spouse, to lift slowly off the ground and fly. They were doubtful, but I told them that (or at least communicated to them that) this was a dream and that almost anything could happen in a dream. I told them to all hold hands in a line and I would lead them.
Conscious of my lucidity, I tried to lift off, but was not successful. I then told myself to relax and then I did a backstroke (as in swimming) and was able to lift off the earth. I then took them up into the air. I had the loose association to the scene in

---

[63] S. Krippner, F. Bogzaran & A. Percia de Carvalho. *Extraordinary Dreams and How to Work with Them*. Albany, NY: State University of New York Press, 2002, p. 43.
[64] S. Krippner & J. Dillard. *Dreamworking, How to Use Your Dreams for Creative Problem-Solving*. Buffalo, NY: Bearly Limited, 1988, p. 183.

"Peter Pan" where someone lifts off the boat or ship of Captain Hook (I saw this in an early T. V. adaptation of "Peter Pan" with Mary Martin in it).

I was aware of needing to maintain lucidity longer in order to prepare for meditation in the lucid state. However, before I got to that the dream content spread out and I lost lucidity.

PMID Step 1: Day-before-dream **event(s)** that connects to this dream.

I, unfortunately, do not recall any day residue from this dream. Wish I did!

PMID Step 2: Day-before-dream **thought(s)** that connect to this dream.

Although I do not recall any day residue for this dream, I do, however, often think of trying to enter lucidity during the night in my daily thoughts. I meditate on this. I believe in the flight of the soul in many ways and disciplines.

PMID Step 3: Major **dream phrases (and symbols)** defined in the context of this dream.

- ***Offered to help the three or four others fly:*** *I am a teacher. This I know. I am aware of my ancestral connections and spiritual responsibilities.*

- ***My spouse:*** *This is my "chosen soul" in this life for better or worse to work through my spiritual evolution.*

- ***Taking them up into the air:*** *(I had the loose association to the scene in "Peter Pan" where someone lifts off the boat or ship of Captain Hook.) I used to want to fly like Peter Pan as a child. Also, African and Caribbean peoples believe souls and people can fly!*

PMID Step 4: Dreaming **emotions** compared with waking life emotions.

I have chosen the role of teacher and guide. What value I do experience derives from helping others. This helps me have a good feeling. It soothes me and provides me with purpose. As a doctor, I help others in waking life. As a father, I try to help and guide my children.

PMID Step 5: Solutions or suggestions for changing thoughts, attitudes or behaviors (answer[s] to day-before-my-dream thoughts).

I can change my attitude and be more open to helping even those who anger me at times. They also want to fly upward. I need to become more patient of others' and my own many shortcomings!

PMID Step 6: Dreaming and waking life **reactions** to each person in this dream.

All the others in the dream are my soul connections. Some I know and love, like my wife. Others are close to me in some way, family and friends, yet their exact connection is a mystery. I need to love the mystery also and fly with the unknown!

Chapter 15

Living Dreams, Living Life, Putting It All Together

We shall not cease from exploration
And the end of all our exploring
Will be to arrive where we started
And know the place for the first time.
  --T. S. Eliot, "Little Gidding," from *Four Quartets*

We experience our daily lives in the context of the whole of our lives. We may or may not see dogs as dangerous, a spouse as loving, or a friend as trustworthy based on a single incident. We are more apt to see from the culmination of experiences.

Dreams are no different. The more we can understand our dreams in the greater context of a *series of dreams* connected to waking life experiences, the more we fully can understand the meaning of our dreams and how, in turn, our dreams can reflect the emotional cinema of our lives.

It is often very helpful for dreamers to go back and review past dreams for reminders and help to understand current dreams. Oftentimes revisiting earlier dreams will reveal hidden meanings that were unclear at the time of the dream. Other times it may be helpful to modify the interpretation of the dream based on hindsight knowledge.

When we neglect to revisit our dreams and interpretations, at least the major ones, we ignore the great reoccurring themes, events, motives, and people who make up this intimate story we call our life.

A few suggestions for when revising dream interpretations

Retain your original dream narrative without change. Changing the dream narrative could eliminate important clues to dream meanings. PMID Step 1: Day-before-dream **event(s)** that connects to this dream and PMID Step 2: Day-before-dream **thought(s)** that connects to this dream **are time-of-the dream facts, so refrain from adding material that you had not recorded somewhere in your interpretations or in a separate journal at the time of your dream.** You might need or want to finesse your previous recordings for Steps 1 and 2 for clarity. You might also want to eliminate time-of-the-dream recordings you later realize are unconnected to your dream.

Naturally, the steps where you will look for possible revisions will be your responses to:
- PMID Step 3: Major dream **phrases (and symbols)** defined in the context of this dream.
- PMID Step 4: Dreaming **emotions** compared with waking life emotions.
- PMID Step 5: **Solution(s)** found by treating dream as answer to pre-dream thoughts (most often day before).
- PMID Step 6: Dreaming and waking life **reactions** to each person in this dream.

For Step 6, also search for whether your current reactions reflect effects from earlier experiences.

Revisiting past dreams for new insights has the potential to reduce repeated messages in future dreams. Repeated dream messages are marvelous though -- when we need them. One circumstance when we need repeated messages is if we have misinterpreted a dream.

Misinterpreting dreams

As we've seen and know from experience, dreams are sometimes misinterpreted. As we've also discussed, revisiting past dreams and working with a series of dreams are the best ways to know that you're on the right track with understanding your dreams.

Summary of how to review your previous interpretations

As you review your original interpretations, re-write them as new insights come. Dreams shed light on one another. So, look to more than one dream about important issues. In addition, when you have misinterpreted an earlier dream, later dreams often point your attention to the earlier misinterpretation.

A productive plan to follow is at the end of every week read through the dreams and interpretations from the week. Then periodically, re-read your dreams and interpretations from months and years previous.

Revisits to our dreams are often excellent helps for becoming familiar with the language of our dreaming minds. You likely will recognize that some of the "language" (your dream phrases and symbols) has appeared in more than one dream.

When you have your dream phrase/symbol directory built up, look for repeated symbols. Review the dream phrase that contains the repeated symbol and trace it to related dreams for whether you have developed differing symbol meanings dependent on the context of your dreams. You could discover as one participant in our studies remarked,

> Since I have begun working on revising my interpretations, I have been amazed at the differences in interpretation of symbols I had after time and reflection. Although on the surface the definitions I first indicated seemed logical, there were also new insights to my symbolic meanings, as well as recognition of additional symbols not previously identified.

As with much of life, when we learn and grow from ongoing experiences we are able to look back at past events with much richer perspectives and deeper understanding. In turn, this new understanding of past events helps clarify and enrich our present lives.

So, too, do our past dreams become richer and fuller of teachings, and the additional knowledge from these greatly expands our understanding and appreciation for our dreams today. Once again, we've learned that, as goes the circle of life, so also does the never-ending circle of our dreams.

Epilogue

No matter what our individual histories, cultures and family backgrounds, it's clear that understanding our dreams is a most profound and effective way to understand ourselves and our lives as has been proven from centuries of ancient philosophical practice through today's modern scientific study. Understanding our dreams *about others,* in particular, is an excellent door through which we arrive at a deeper understanding *of ourselves.*

You can interpret your dreams about others since you now hold the resources for understanding your dreams. Those resources are the ability to recall day-before-the-dream events, thoughts, and emotions that will connect you to your dream, and the ability to realize that your personal experiences largely create your dream language. Those resources, together with the staying power to revisit dreams for new insights, are what you need to begin using this system.

As you use these resources, we trust you will find -- perhaps already have found -- that your dreaming mind is an almost infinite reservoir to help you discover and build the relationships of which you have always dreamed. Enjoy your journey. We trust you will be amazed.

Dream on!

Evelyn M. Duesbury, MS Counselor Education
  Member of the American Counselor Association
  Member of the American Psychological Association

  Other books by Duesbury:

The Counselor's Guide for Facilitating the Interpretation of Dreams: Family and Other Relationship Systems Perspectives. (November 2010). New York: Routledge

A Dream-Guided Meditation Model and the Personalized Method For Interpreting Dreams. (2017). New York: Routledge.

Writers' Guiding Dreams. (2018). Spain: Editorial Calliope.

TABLE

Personalized Method for Interpreting Dreams (PMID) Steps

PMID Step 1: Record the **event(s)** you had before your dream (most often, day before) that appears either objectively or figuratively in this dream.

PMID Step 2: Record the **thought(s)** you had before your dream (most often, day before) that seem to connect to this dream either objectively or figuratively. Write "I thought" statements to help clarify which day-before-the-dream thoughts brought this dream.

PMID Step 3: Select and define **major dream phrases** and symbols from your write-up of this dream to discover the dream's personalized meanings. Consider effects of day-before-your dream events, thoughts, and earlier experiences on the meaning of each major dream phrase and symbol. The general definition for "phrases" as used in this step is "a string of words." The strings of words can be phrases, clauses, or whole sentences.

PMID Step 4: Compare your dreaming **emotions** with your waking life emotions about the main issue and/or relationship in this dream. What differences, if any, do you find between your dreaming emotions and waking life emotions? Also, periodically review your dreaming emotions about the main issue or relationship.

PMID Step 5: Explore your dream for possible **solutions or suggestions** on changing thoughts, attitudes or behaviors (answer[s] to day-before-my-dream thoughts).

PMID Step 6: With whom is your primary **relationship** in this dream? Compare your dreaming and waking life **reactions** to each person in this dream. In addition, note any influences from the past indicated in this dream.

Appendix 1

Dream Phrase Directory (and Symbols) (Compilation of dreamers' personal definitions)

Bathroom stool in front office: Foremost importance of letting go of no longer useable products, such as thoughts and emotions, in dealing with relationship issues I thought about last night.

Best to room with Barbara: Best to stay with my highest appraisal of myself to overcome self-doubt feelings I had yesterday. Barbara's friendship helps my self-worth feelings.

Curls not permanent: My dreaming mind adds the wisdom that the curls in the hair "thought influence" isn't a permanent influence on my wife. Hair often represents thoughts since hair comes from the head.

Death of hyperactive family member: Have overcome tendency to become hyperactive during social conversations, affirming my calm feeling from visit yesterday

Decide to be friendly with person: Way to overcome stressful emotions about the person in this dream is to think friendly thoughts about her.

Difficult person being just nice: Her presence in my mother-in-law's house, being friendly and just nice -- no hint of her difficult personality I had previously experienced -- reveals my changed thoughts and feelings toward my mother-in-law.

Distressed that Roswell going to marry Geraldine: Putdown that stems from feeling putdown during young adulthood when Roswell's choice of friends didn't include me. Response to my pre-dream question of what Roswell means in my dreams.

Does not want to hear what I have to say: Be cautious about remorseful reminiscing. In the dream, a childhood friend thinks I am going to talk about activities in which she might have been involved. Last night I almost went into talking remorsefully about this friend.

Father is sick: Weakness will result in my normally healthy-mindedness if I continue to omit my usual "inner listening timeouts." My father sometimes represents need for inner listening.

Feet do not touch the floor: Not doing my part in a waking life venture. The man I dance with during my dream is a waking life associate.

Finally leave Joleatha and bring my spouse home: Successful overcoming of unfounded worries about whether my spouse was upset last night. Joleatha grossly overreacts.

Fluorescent bulb handed to hyperactive relative: Responds to my thoughts about impulsive comments I made yesterday and tells me to make my responses slower and less intense. Florescent bulbs light up slower and are not as hot as regular bulbs.

Go swimming after Eleanoise leaves: Way to escape from downcast feelings I had periodically yesterday (symbolized by Eleanoise in this dream) is to sink into the pool of my inner resources.

Grade of one millionth of a point: Essay I prepared yesterday is very poorly done.

Have a baby for her: Person wants help with bringing birth to the meaning of her dreams, which responds to my yesterday's thoughts of whether this person is serious about dreamwork.

Hold bathed child up for spouse to see: Response to my last night's sense of relief from spouse and my meshing very well on topic that was touchy in the past.

Increasingly see more dirt: The more I view our interactions with Mom as negative, the more negative the situation seems to me.

Intentionally close the door: Closed the door to a matter that is now dead, is now over.

Key hanging from the locked door: There is some key in this dream of how to relieve stress from the disagreement with my spouse last night. The door in the dream is to my spouse's office.

Lion has done battle: Symbolic of experiences during my early spiritual pursuits. I had some experiences that interfered with instead of promoted my spiritual understanding. (Lion -- "In ancient Christian symbolism the lion represented Jesus. . . 'Lion of Judah' [Christ]," Boushahla & Reidel-Geubtner, 1992, 105).

Lost my personal computer: What often happens to me when I am with people like those in this dream. I lose my own best thoughts and react very poorly.

Machine in office not turned off: Responds to my last night's anxious thoughts about upcoming projects and shows why I had difficulty getting to sleep.

Marry friend's spouse: Will need commitment from the spouse of the friend I drafted a letter to last night, so rephrase the letter to include the spouse.

Meticulous garden work: Answers my last night's thoughts about a co-worker and assures me that he does extremely thorough work.

Missed our very fine little girl friendship: Lets me know the true way I felt about losing a childhood friend who was in an earlier dream that I reviewed last night.

Mom urging me to dress well: After working through mothering issues, get on with wearing those fine personality characteristics.

My car doing a little chugging: In the dream I say that pieces of my teeth (speech) falling out likely is the cause of the car difficulty. Comes from my day before the dream pessimistic thoughts and words and subsequent inability to relax my body "vehicle" into sleep

My room in parents' house under construction: Relationship dreams I worked with yesterday will have constructive influence on my childhood impressions.

No intercourse: No current working connection between the person represented in the dream and myself unless I take a more active part.

Parents providing step-upped food: Working through relationship concerns about parents provides increasingly higher quality "food" for personality development.

Person changes into a different person: Woman I thought about yesterday will be unreceptive to what I planned to write to her, even though she asked me to write. In the dream, she stiffens and changes into an uptight person I know.

Pool washing my hair: Pool of inner resources cleanses thoughts. Hair often symbolizes thoughts (universal meaning).

Problem giving up child after I give birth: Caution about continuing emotional connection to another's work after the person is past needing my help.

Pulling weeds out of in-law's flowerbed: Get rid of negative thoughts that surfaced yesterday about this in-law, thus avoid smothering my positive thoughts about her.

Pulls out a gun: A person's negative responses to me last night felt more threatening than I realized.

Pumping too much gas into family's car: I talked too much to my family -- gassed (talked) too much about an interview I had yesterday.

Purse here every time I check: Wavering confidence that I felt yesterday about my talents (money in my purse) is unfounded.

Recognize not enough room for me between dad and sons: Becoming aware, either in the dream, or consciously, there no longer is room for me to be the center of attention or to be between my husband and our sons.

Sister's pool near house: Ready access to diving into refreshing thoughts about sister we contacted yesterday.

Snake I am doing surgery on: Could represent my spiritual nature. Prompted by my notice of the clay snake on our dresser yesterday and yesterday reading that Jung referred to the serpent as a spiritual sign.

Snake over my legs holding me down: Chairperson of the committee meeting I plan to attend today will counter my proposals and restrict me from moving in the direction I think best.

Spiritual teacher running into trouble near the cornfield: Reflects a traumatic scene from early adulthood, possibly to show I hurt my spiritual understanding by meddling in my dad's life.

Spiritual teacher to work in my dad's fields: My biological father is taking on a new representation in some of my dreams. I believe my dream's reference to "my father's fields" is symbolic of God. For most of my early life, I called God, "Father."

Stitching the sock end up right away: Mimic of my mom-in-law's doing mending "right now" means mend the irritated feelings I felt last night. Stitch in time to avoid more stitches later.

Teeth chipped off: Self-blaming I did yesterday is affecting my good quality speech (teeth). In the dream and in waking life I had little concern about the effect on me. Yet, my dream cautions me there is concern.

Turning into Swinerath's drive: Stop turning thoughts into pessimism, which is what I did yesterday after first discovering a golden opportunity and then kicking myself in afterthought that I might have actually messed it up. (I think of pessimism when I think of Mr. Swinerath.)

Two different types of birds flying well together: Answers my thoughts of whether a person and I will work well together. Although different personality types, we will work well together.

Ugly underpants showing below nice shorts: Letter I wrote last night has some heavy undertones that I will not be able to hide if I send it.

Walk way home myself: In the context of my yesterday's thoughts, I need to stay close to my fine feelings of self-worth that my friend in the dream inspired in me.

Walking with Clarion: Comes from my thought last night to ease work on my favorite project in favor of taking time to socialize more like Clarion does, something I do not want to do.

Wall connected with crying-moaning: Oh, wailing wall. Going to wail about a past circumstance that I thought about last night. Caution.

Want person to know grief caused me: Dream reveals I still want to blame the other for my grief reactions to a past event, an event I thought about last night.

Wants me to dust picture of Dad: Brother's dream request to dust picture of Dad reminds me that the inspirational words I read last night connect to our dad's emotional nature.

Won game in the 13th Inning: Triumphed over obstacles I faced yesterday.

Words on fantail of an Eagle in flight: Connects to my day before the dream thoughts about a project and shows that the project will fly quite successfully.

===================================

Appendix 2

Research and Explorations of the Personalized Method for Interpreting Dreams (PMID)

In this appendix, we present synopses of our research and explorations to give you an idea of the PMID model's development and to give you confidence in the PMID process.

Researches and explorations were all conducted through the University of Wisconsin-Whitewater, Counselor Education Department. Each project was at least three months long, all with small samples ranging from 8 – 11 *active* (contributions to conclusion) participants. The two most important factors that motivated our research of the Personalized Method for Interpreting Dreams (PMID) are first, research of dream interpretation models is sparse, and second, there is limited training in dream interpretation models for professionals. Lack of research naturally contributes to lack of training.

Results first shown are from Duesbury's thesis research (2000) that culminated in the Personalized Method for Interpreting Dreams (PMID). Following that are results from Van Doren and Duesbury's pilot study (2000), Van Doren and Duesbury's explorations (2001), Duesbury, Bynum, and Van Doren's explorations (2002, 2003), Van Doren and Duesbury's research of ongoing use of the PMID (2005-2006), and Okocha and Duesbury's research of the general population's ability to use the PMID model (2005-2006).

Assessment instruments we developed and used are shown at the end of this appendix.

Thesis Case Study

The thesis committee was composed of Brenda O'Beirne, Ph.D., Aneneosa Okocha, Ph.D., and David Van Doren, Ed. D., counselor education department. Outcomes of this study in relation to the five research questions posed are all positive. The Personalized Method for Interpreting Dreams (PMID) was found to be useful for self-facilitation (Research Question 1). All six steps in the Personalized Method for Interpreting Dreams were found to be uniquely personal to the case study participant (Research Question 2). Use of dream interpretations reflected change in affect (emotions) over time (Research Question 3), and use of the dream interpretations helped the participant understand and mollify her relationship issues (Research Questions 4 and 5) (Duesbury, 2000, 2001). The case study thesis participant "Rose" volunteered series of dreams about seven relationships in her life. Though none of the series covered seven years, the "package" of dreams did span seven years. She wrote --

> As I came to understand and feel relief from stress in any one relationship, it helped me understand and feel relief from stress with other relationships.
>
> I must tell you I worked very hard to learn the language of my dreams although it is my own personal language. I didn't learn in a flash. For me it took dedicated recording of dreams and intuitive insight to achieve fruitful dream interpretations.

Robert L. Van de Castle, Ph. D. (author of *Our Dreaming Mind*, 1994 and respected researcher) rated thesis case study participant's 70 dream interpretations (seven series of dreams, averaging ten dreams per series). He appraised that she had reduced stress about all seven people she dreamed about.

Van Doren-Duesbury (Summer 2000) -- Research

The purposes of the study were to: (1) Examine the ability of counselor education graduates and current graduate students, facilitated by a dreamwork teacher, to use the PMID Personalized Method for Interpreting Dreams, and (2) Test the functionality of the web site to collect and store data (applications, pre-tests, dream reports, and interpretations). Because researchers required an excessive number of relationship type dreams (seven) from each participant before giving them access to the PMID model (for pre-testing purposes), the research period ended before most participants received the PMID model. Some relationship issues identified in participants' interpretations (Non-PMID and PMID) were:

- Spouse: distrust of, disagreements with, divorced, deceased
- Marriage: breakup, new marriage
- Significant other: difficulty in gay relationships, breakup, emotional ties to former partner
- Parents: restrictive, reluctance to rely on family and friends, alcoholic family members
- Sexual molestation

As expected, the beta test of the web site developed for this pilot study successfully accommodated data input, data retention, and data exploration.

Van Doren-Duesbury (Summer 2001) -- Explorations

Duesbury and Van Doren observed that volunteers (composed of some Wisconsin Counseling Association members and some UW-Whitewater counseling education graduates) using the Personalized Method for Interpreting Dreams (PMID) for the first time were able to reduce stress about relationship concerns within two months of learning the PMID model. Ability to understand and use the PMID model to reduce stressful feelings within a short time supports use of the PMID for brief counseling applications. Volunteers for learning the PMID model presented dreams that included members of their families of origin. These are classic dreams that encourage the dreamer to revisit early experiences to understand how early experiences might affect current reactions, the systemic effects.

Robert Van de Castle, Ph. D. (respected researcher) rated the six active participants' dream interpretations before and after they learned the PMID model. His ratings were as follows (the first percentage is before, and the second percentage is after): Connect events to dreams 76.9%, 100%; Connect thoughts to dreams 7.7%, 100%; Define dream phrases 0%, 66.7%; Recognize dreaming emotions 92.3%, 95.8%; Found suggestions or solutions in dreams 23.1%, 100%; Explored dream reactions to others 69.2%, 87.5%. Duesbury and Van Doren's examinations of the participants' dreams and interpretations support these statistics.

Duesbury-Bynum-Van Doren (Fall 2002 and Fall 2003) -- Explorations

Our experiences with first-time users of the Personalized Method for Interpretation Dreams (PMID) in two counselor education graduate level dream interpretation classes showed high ability to use the PMID model from within a few weeks to a couple months of learning the PMID model. Almost all users we observed self-reported positive change about one or more relationships during a timeframe of between a few weeks to two months. Most self-rated their use of the PMID steps prior to learning the PMID model very low and after several weeks of using the PMID model, rated their ability to do all six steps very high. We used the Wilcoxon's Repeated Measures Signed-Ranks test of significance to analyze the self-ratings. For instance, during explorations of one class of students, the probability at eight weeks was $W- = 1, W+ = 65, N = 11, p <= 0.001953$ that these same positive results would have been attained simply by chance. At 14 weeks the probability remained stable at the significant levels achieved by eight weeks.

Van Doren-Duesbury (2005-2006) -- Research

In this study, we found that ongoing abilities to use the PMID model varied only minimally from the time of learning the PMID model to three years later. Evidence was provided by seven former counselor education graduate level students who volunteered either self-reported ratings of their ability to do the PMID steps, and/or dreams and interpretations.

Okocha-Duesbury (2005-2006–six months) -- Research General Population

We asked volunteers from the general population who continued active participation for six-month to rate their "before-after" abilities to do each PMID step, using a 7-point scale (1=low, 7=high). Mean rating from before using the PMID model was 2.88 and mean rating at the conclusion was 6.06. Using the Wilcoxon's Repeated Measures Signed-Ranks test of significance to analyze participants' responses, we found a probability of $p <= 0.007812$ that these same positive results would have been attained by chance. Our reviews of the eight six-month active participants' interpretations support their increasing success shown in these statistics.

Facilitative comments from the co-investigator on participants' use of the PMID model appeared to be an important factor in increasing ability to use the PMID model. We presented the following "Yes-No" statement at the end of the study: "Comments from Evelyn were more helpful than I could have done on my own". 100% of the respondents indicated a response of "Yes".

Assessment Instruments Used: <u>**Instrument No. 1 – Screening Application**</u>

Personal Information

Date Applied:	Gender:
Username:	Birthday:
Password:	Occupation:
First and Last Name:	Highest Level of
Address:	Education completed
Phone:	Degree/Major
Email:	Marital Status
	Ethnicity:

Self Rating *(Scale 1-7 with 7 high)*
   <u>Question and Rating</u>
1. My current ability to understand my dream symbols:
2. My ability to solve puzzles:
3. My ability to learn new skills as:
4. My interest in this research is to try to help me relieve stress:
5. I wonder if my past relationships affect how I function in my current relationships.
6. Overall, I'm very happy with my level of "success" in life:

Multiple Choice (Mark Yes [Y] for all that apply for each statement.)

1. I currently
   ☐ Am not involved with working with my dreams
   ☐ Would like to learn how to find personal meanings in my dreams
   ☐ Use a dream interpretation method that seems to be helpful
   ☐ Use a dream interpretation method that does NOT seem to be helpful
   ☐ Am involved in dream study with an individual counselor
   ☐ Am involved in dream study with a group counselor
   ☐ Am involved with self-help dream interpretation on a regular basis

2. I recall my dreams
   - ☐ Every night
   - ☐ Two or more times a week
   - ☐ About once a week
   - ☐ Rarely
   - ☐ Rarely, but I would like to recall them more

3. I am:
   - ☐ A dream researcher myself and interested in what others are doing
   - ☐ A dream researcher and am searching for more effective dreamwork methods
   - ☐ Interested because I teach dream studies and/or related areas
   - ☐ I am a counselor or therapist
   - ☐ An individual interested in learning how to interpret my dreams

4. I am a:
   - ☐ Self-starter
   - ☐ Procrastinator
   - ☐ Procrastinator, unless I am involved in a learning and creative activity

5. My friends describe me as:
   - ☐ Reliable
   - ☐ Energetic
   - ☐ Honest
   - ☐ A loner
   - ☐ Interested in self-improvement
   - ☐ Competitive
   - ☐ Logical and reasoning
   - ☐ Intuitive
   - ☐ Patient
   - ☐ Creative
   - ☐ Prompt

6. I describe myself as:
   - ☐ A happy person
   - ☐ Motivated to work out my problems
   - ☐ A person who has difficulty getting started with projects and other responsibilities
   - ☐ A person who does things that keeps my interested
   - ☐ A person who has, at times, had weeks or months of being unable to take care of my daily tasks
   - ☐ A brooding person
   - ☐ Not as good as other people

7. Lately I have thought a lot about:
   - ☐ Wishing I were dead, but I would not kill myself
   - ☐ Wishing I were dead, and how I would kill myself
   - ☐ Life in the hereafter
   - ☐ Other similar topics

8. Lately I often feel:
   - ☐ Lonely
   - ☐ Blue
   - ☐ Happy
   - ☐ Useless
   - ☐ Energetic
   - ☐ That I don't care what happens to me

9. It seems to me that:
   - ☐ Most people don't care what happens to me
   - ☐ Life is worthwhile

10. My future seems:
    - ☐ Bright
    - ☐ Hopeless
    - ☐ Empty and meaningless
    - ☐ Uncertain, but hopeful

11. I am familiar with the following dream interpretation methods:
    - ☐ Jungian
    - ☐ Perls
    - ☐ Freudian
    - ☐ PMID
    - ☐ Other

12. I am currently taking medications:
    - ☐ Yes
    - ☐ No

13. I am:
    - ☐ In a long-term intimate relationship with a spouse
    - ☐ In a long-term intimate relationship with a partner
    - ☐ In an intimate relationship with a significant other person
    - ☐ Am not currently in a long-term intimate relationship
    - ☐ Have never been in a long-term intimate relationship

Essay (Write in the blanks)

1. The activity I most enjoy is:
2. The relationship that I seem to dream the most about (living or passed on) is:
3. Other major relationships that I seem to dream the most about (living or passed on) are:
4. The one greatest success I am currently experiencing is:
5. Other sources of success I am currently experiencing are:
6. The one greatest frustration I am currently experiencing is with:
7. Other sources of frustration I am currently experiencing are:
8. Summing it all up, the reasons I want to participate in this project with particular focus on relationship issues are:

©2004 Evelyn M. Duesbury and David Van Doren, All rights reserved.

Instrument No. 2 - Periodic Feedback Instrument (PFI)

On a scale of 1-7 (1 = Strongly Disagree and 7 = Strongly Agree) using the Personalized Method for Interpreting Dreams (PMID), I rate my ability to:
1. Connect my waking life events (most often those occurring the day before) to my dreams.
2. Connect my waking life thoughts (most often those occurring the day before) to my dreams.
3. Develop personal definitions for dream phrases (and symbols), in the context of this dream.
4. Identify when my dreaming emotions and waking life emotions are similar and when they are different about the main issue in the dream.
5. Discover problem-solving suggestions that answer my day-before-the-dream thoughts.
6. Compare my reactions in relationship experiences as reflected in this dream with my waking life reactions in similar circumstances.

(Nos. 1-5 are for all dreams; No. 6 is only for relationship dreams)
Comments: _____
   ©Evelyn M. Duesbury

Instrument No. 3 - Emotional Change Instrument

1. Of the dreams and PMID interpretations I have entered at this point, I have noticed a difference in my dreaming emotions from my waking emotions about a situation for at least one of my dreams and interpretations. Yes ___ No ___. If yes, my title(s) for the dream(s) is (are): _____
2. The number of dreams and PMID interpretations I have entered at this point are _____. If one or more, continue to 3 and 4.
3. Of the dreams and PMID interpretations I have entered at this point I have recorded emotions in the dream narrative itself for _____ of those dreams.

4. Of the dreams and PMID interpretations I have entered at this point I have dreamed more than once about at least one relationship. Yes____ No _____ If yes, continue to 5 and 6

5. The relationship(s) I have dreamed about more than once at this point is (are): _____

6. I have noticed a positive change in my dreaming emotions about one or more relationships.

    Yes___No ___. If yes, continue to 7

7. Title(s) of my dreams where I have noticed a positive change in my dreaming emotions about one or more relationships are (is):

_____

Comments: _____
©Evelyn M. Duesbury

In summary, our research and observations showed that participants' aptitude for intuitive insight combined with rational reasoning were primary characteristics for achieving success with the PMID model. We found intuitive awareness was not only a helpful characteristic for working with dreams, but also found indications of intuitive awareness being increased when using the PMID model.

Appendix 3

International Association for the Study of Dreams

The International Association for the Study of Dreams is a non-profit, international, multidisciplinary organization dedicated to the pure and applied investigation of dreams and dreaming.

The purposes of this organization are to promote an awareness and appreciation of dreams in both professional and public arenas; to encourage research into the nature, function, and significance of dreaming; to advance the application of the study of dreams; and to provide a forum for the eclectic and interdisciplinary exchange of ideas and information. (http://www.asdreams.org)

Appendix 4

Suggested Exercises for Chapters 1 through 15

Chapter 1 -- Preliminary Work: Write down the events that happened in your life yesterday and last evening. Now see if any of those events connect to a dream you had during the night last night. Connections could be either symbolic or objective.

Chapter 2 -- PMID Step 1: Write one dream on paper! Write the dream exactly as you recall it. Notice that writing makes the dream clearer than just thinking about it, and it also retains the dream. Record day-before-your dream event(s) that could connect to your dream.

Chapter 3 -- PMID Step 2: Practice is gratifying! Write another dream on paper! Also, write the first two clues (day-before-the-dream events and thoughts). Whoops, do you only recall a fragment of a dream? Fragments can be helpful -- sometimes *very* helpful. Record the fragment. Connect it to a day-before-the-dream thought(s) and a day-before-the-dream event(s).

Chapter 4 -- PMID Step 3: Review the Dream Phrase Directory in Appendix 1. If you care to, make a file of all the personal dream phrases/symbols you have defined so far for your dreams.

Chapter 5 -- PMID Step 4: As you keep a running journal of your dreams, we suggest that you watch the emotional monitors guiding you onward. Surprised? Or Whoops -- did you forget to write your dreaming emotions within your dream narratives? In any event, record emotions within your next dream narratives.

Chapter 6 -- PMID Step 5: Before you act on what you believe are insights and/or direct solutions in your dreams, "Listen" in an intuitive mode for whether the solutions you find seem accurate. When correct, you could even have a confirming feel within your body. For critical matters look to more than one dream and consider visiting with a trusted friend or counselor.

Chapter 7 -- PMID Step 6: As you read dreamer Alice's PMID interpretations, notice she traced earlier experiences to her current reactions. Take a *closer* look at *your relationship dreams and interpretations* to help you discover insights about how you might be reacting currently to others based on your earlier experiences.

Chapter 8 -- Dreams about Parents: Review some of your own dreams about your parents if you have dreams about your parents. Notice possible healthy and possible unhealthy reactions. Ponder whether dreams about deceased parents could be helpful to you.

Chapter 9 -- Coincidence of Psi-dreams of Marital Pair, Same Night Dreams: Think about the phenomena of people dreaming similar dreams on the same night and whether such occurrences provide support that dream content is influenced by more than random firings in the brain.

Chapter 10 -- Victorious Handling of Situations: Ponder whether you have had dream confirmation for a job well done in pulling yourself up from otherwise discouraging circumstances.

Chapter 11 -- Facing Nightmares and Scary Dreams. Facing Life: Think about your dreaming -- and whether any of your dreams classify as scary dreams. We believe there is something good about every dream. Even so, be cautious about moving too rapidly onward when you have scary dreams.

Chapter 12 -- Everyday Dreams. Everyday Life: If you dreamed about an everyday activity that you did or thought about yesterday, write it down on paper! Also, before you forget them record day-before-the-dream events and thoughts that could connect to your dream plus your day-before-the-dream waking-life emotions about the main topic of your dream. Record these important clues now in order to retain them.

Chapter 13 -- Spiritual Dreams. Spiritual Life: Examine one of your spiritual-type dreams for whether it has relationship-type symbolism in it. Examine some of your relationship-type dreams for whether any have spiritual-type symbolism in them.

Chapter 14 -- Lucid Dreams. Living Dreams: Ponder, "Why on earth would you want to let the 'Cognitive Sensor' manipulate your dreams?" Then ponder whether lucid dreaming brings "excitement, delight, and knowledge" unmatched by ordinary dreams. Each person must decide for himself or herself on the merits of lucid dreaming.

Chapter 15 -- Living Life. Putting It All Together: As you finish reading this book, start an enjoyable routine designed for you to increase your productive use of the Personalized Method for Interpreting Dreams (PMID): At the end of each week review your dreams and PMID interpretations for that week. At the same time, list your dream titles in a separate file, in date order. Periodically review the titles for dreams you want to inspect closer. Expect your dedication to pay off in fruitful use of your dreams, and consequently time saved in the longer term.

Appendix 5

Historical Perspectives and Some Contemporary Dream Interpretation Models

All of us dream every night of our lives, as has every human since the dawn of humankind. Until about 400 years ago dreams and their meanings played hugely significant roles in nearly every culture around the globe since the dawn of civilization. Bynum, a dream researcher, has suggested, along with many others, that every culture has had "individual, family, and divine or spiritual dreams" at the roots since the dawn of its very existence.[65]

Dreams of the ancients

Dr. Robert Van de Castle has worked with dreams and dreaming for many years, including authoring a landmark book on the topic.[66] His findings on ancient cultural use of dreams reveal a widespread dependence on dream guidance. Incubation, a focusing process to invite dreams about specific topics, was a common practice in several ancient cultures, as was the belief that rulers and prophets were the predominant recipients of dreams.

The Hebrew prophets looked to their dreams to guide their people, as well as to interpret Gentile rulers' dreams. The ancient Hebrew people were freed from Egyptian slavery as a result of Daniel and Joseph's interpretation of rulers' dreams. The Hebrews attributed the source of their dreams to God, one god alone, while the Egyptians attributed the source of their dreams to many different gods all dwelling within the One God.

The ancient Chinese connected their dreams to daytime words and thoughts, and India's Upanishads connected early childhood dreams with the dreamer's previous lives and later adulthood dreams to future lives.

---

[65] E. B. Bynum. *Families and the Interpretation of Dreams: Awakening the Intimate Web.* Paraview Books, 2003, p. 28.
[66] R. L. Van de Castle. *Our Dreaming Mind.* New York: Ballantine Books, 1994.

The early Greeks' appreciation for the power of dreams is reflected in Homer's heroes and in Hippocrates' medical practices. These Greek dreamwork practices were in themselves built largely upon earlier Egyptian ones, then spread to the Greeks and Romans, taking on a local coloring as they progressed. The practices of dream interpretation and divination were closely connected and widely embraced throughout the Mediterranean at all levels of society. Not everyone accepted this, of course. Cicero rejected the idea of dream credibility.[67]

Krippner, et al.[68] reports that cultural beginnings can be traced to the base of many major religions. For examples, the *Talmud* and the *Bible*'s *Old Testament* contain many dream guidance accounts.

Van de Castle[69] recognizes some "giant" dreamworkers from the past; one is the North African scholar Synesius of Cyrene who lived in the fifth-century AD. Synesius "was a fervent proponent of the many practical applications to be derived from cultivating dreams."[70] Among Synesius' practical applications was his conviction that people should explore the personal meanings in their dream symbols instead of consulting dream books for interpretations. Exploring the personal meanings in dreams is gaining momentum in current times and is a tradition we follow in this book.

Another of Synesius' practices that is gaining momentum in current times is his passionate exploration of dreams for the inspirational joy of spiritual communication. Alas, no one carried Synesius' pioneering work on to the West in subsequent centuries until Morton Kelsey (twentieth century Episcopal minister) discovered omission of Synesius' works from English texts.[71]

---

[67] R. L. Van de Castle. *Our Dreaming Mind*. New York: Ballantine Books, 1994.
[68] S. Krippner, C. Jaeger, & L. Faith. "Identifying and Utilizing Spiritual Content in Dream Reports," *Dreaming 11*(3), 2001, pp. 127-147.
[69] R. L. Van de Castle. *Our Dreaming Mind*. New York: Ballantine Books, 1994.
[70] R. L. Van de Castle. *Our Dreaming Mind*. New York: Ballantine Books, 1994, p. 76.
[71] R. L. Van de Castle. *Our Dreaming Mind*. New York: Ballantine Books, 1994.

Africa has a "long cultural, clinical, and psychospiritual history" in family dreaming that extends to contemporary times.[72] Many African spiritual groups believe that living and deceased family members, as well as the older ancestral spirits, appear in dreams and give guidance.

Extensive groups of Native Americans often acted on dream guidance from guardian spirits.[73] Australian Aboriginals have developed a dreamwork method based on the belief that the dreamer takes a journey and in the process receives guidance for specific purposes, such as healing, finding food, and gaining spiritual enrichment.[74]

The ancient Chinese used dreams for diagnostic purposes, a practice that continues in modern times. Middle Eastern cultures developed ritual prayers to keep "negative forces" from influencing them through their dreams and through their waking life. The Muslims of Islam developed ritual prayers to stimulate responding dreams. Japan's tradition of dream interpretation is based on Japanese Buddhism and Shinto and, like several other early religions, "focuses on the worship of and devotion to deities of natural forces."[75]

Nevertheless, influential people changed dreamwork practices in major world cultures. Kelsey[76] explains that the original Christians depended most on dreams for communication with God until during the Enlightenment (seventeenth and eighteenth centuries) when people were swayed into believing that spiritual contact was impossible.

Although Jerome (fourth century translator) had dramatic dream insights himself, for unknown reasons he later mistranslated dream for the Hebrew word <u>anan</u> (soothsayer or witch) several times when he

---

[72] E. B. Bynum. *Families and the Interpretation of Dreams: Awakening the Intimate Web.* Paraview Books, 2003, p. 30.

[73] Kilborne, cited in E. B. Bynum, *Families and the Interpretation of Dreams: Awakening the Intimate Web.* Paraview Books, 2003.

[74] E. B. Bynum. *Families and the Interpretation of Dreams: Awakening the Intimate Web.* Paraview Books, 2003.

[75] E. B. Bynum.. *Families and the Interpretation of Dreams: Awakening the Intimate Web.* Paraview Books, 2003.

[76] M. Kelsey. *God, Dreams and Revelation: A Christian Interpretation of Dreams.* Minneapolis: Augsburg, 1991.

translated the Bible from Hebrew and Greek to Latin.[77] Van de Castle[78] declares that Jerome's mistranslation, combined with other Church discredits of dreamwork, held dreamwork in disfavor for fifteen centuries.

In the thirteenth century, emphasis placed Saint Thomas Aquinas' Aristotelian ideas that only holy and important people had dreams of divine origin and that conscious thought is superior to reasoning done while asleep also diminished credibility for dreamwork.[79] This "one-sided interpretation of Thomas Aquinas"[80] contributed to devaluing dreams.

As stated above, some dreamwork practices that were restricted are finding their way back to common usage. Interest in dream guidance is reflected in the increasing number of national dreamwork organizations. For examples, Austria, Australia, Belgium, Brazil, Bulgaria, Chile, China, Denmark, England, France, Germany, Greece, Italy, Ireland, Japan, Mexico, Netherlands, New Zealand, Russia, Switzerland and the United States of America all have established national dreamwork organizations.

In our view, the potential that dream insights have to balance the personality is a major reason for the current growing interest in dream guidance. This current growing interest in dreams represents a "recovery" from another significant interruption in the appreciation for dreams -- an interruption felt especially in the Western World.

During the middle and later parts of the twentieth century, the scientific method of discovery revolutionized the "civilized" world. However, emphasis on objective evidence and mistrust of anything subjective diminished credibility for dreamwork.[81]

More recently, qualitative research methods are increasingly accepted and, as a result, at least some researchers are recognizing dreams as trustworthy evidence.

---

[77] M. Kelsey. *God, Dreams and Revelation: A Christian Interpretation of Dreams.* Minneapolis: Augsburg, 1991.
[78] R. L. Van de Castle. *Our Dreaming Mind.* New York: Ballantine Books, 1994.
[79] R. L. Van de Castle. *Our Dreaming Mind.* New York: Ballantine Books, 1994.
[80] M. Kelsey. *God, Dreams and Revelation: A Christian Interpretation of Dreams.* Minneapolis: Augsburg, 1991, p. 8.
[81] M. Kelsey. *Transcend, a Guide to the Spiritual Quest.* New York: Crossroad, 1981.

Bulkeley[82] describes some classification systems people from several cultures have developed and then he comments,

> Looking at these different classification systems, we can draw some general conclusions regarding what humans dream about. People dream about their daily experiences, their bodies, their relations with other people, their fears and wishes, their future, and their relations with the sacred.

From dreams to discoveries

The contribution of dreams to the work of scientists, musicians and other artists and the related impact on society throughout history have had is tremendous. Dreams gave Kekule the closed ring structure of the benzene molecule, Frederick Banting instructions on how to isolate the insulin hormone and the list goes on and on.

As just a few of the countless examples:

Dreams give inventors solutions.
Mendeleyev in 1869, working on a way to categorize the chemical elements based on their atomic weights dreamed the table that resulted in the periodic table of elements. In his dream, "all the elements fell into place as required"; in only one place he felt a correction was necessary. All the rest Mendeleyev retained as he recorded from his dream.[83]

Dreams give composers music.
En route to Vienna in 1821, Beethoven dozed in his carriage and dreamed he was on a different journey -- one to the Middle East. As he wandered through desert scenery, he heard an exotic canon playing -- not exactly Middle Eastern music, but it was nevertheless unusual and enticing. "Scarcely did I awake when away flew the canon," he lamented, "and I could not recall any part of it." On returning from Vienna the next

---

[82] K. Bulkeley. *Spiritual Dreaming, A Cross-Cultural and Historical Journey*. New Jersey: Paulist Press, 1992.
[83] Cited in R. L. Van de Castle. (1994). *Our Dreaming Mind.* New York: Ballantine Books, 1994, p. 35.

day in the same carriage, the composer found himself in a reverie about the previous day's lost music. In this state, close to sleep, with all the situational cues at hand, he heard the same music "as fast as Menelaus did Proteus" and transcribed it exactly. He later made only three changes in his symphony.[84]

Singer/songwriter Billy Joel gets nightly memos from the Committee of Sleep. "I always dream music," he reports. "I know all the music I've composed has come from a dream."[85]

Joseph Shabalala, founder of Ladysmith Black Mambazo and composer of two tracks on Paul Simon's Grammy Award-winning album *Graceland,* also hears all his compositions in dreams. He reports he's dreamed music every night of his life, always sung by a choir of children.[86]

Dreams give horticulturists ideas for new plant varieties.
Luther Burbank developed many new varieties of fruits, vegetables, and flowers, including the Burbank potato and the Shasta daisy. He never mentioned dreams in his three books; however, Burbank's secretary, Mildred Hirschberg, reported that he wrote all of his dreams down. As they occurred through the night, he jotted them down telegraphically on bits of scrap paper and tossed them on the floor as he returned to sleep. Mrs. Hirschberg was assigned the task of going through his quarters, gathering these up each day, and typing out their contents. She reported that they looked like "mostly nonsense" to her, but Burbank studied them carefully and said that many of his best plant ideas came from them.[87]

A childhood dream gave Einstein inspiration for the Theory of Relativity. Following is an excerpt from a May 1998 letter written to me by Eileen Riordan, former Jungian Dream Workshop Presenter:

---

[84] Cited in D. Barrett. *The Committee of Sleep.* Crown Publishers, NY, 2001, pp. 68-69.
[85] Cited in D. Barrett. *The Committee of Sleep.* Crown Publishers, NY, 2001, p. 71.
[86] Cited in D. Barrett. *The Committee of Sleep.* Crown Publishers, NY, 2001, p. 72.
[87] Cited in D. Barrett. *The Committee of Sleep.* Crown Publishers, NY, 2001, p. 115.

Towards his later years, Einstein was being interviewed by Edwin Newmann. Newmann asked him how he got the inspiration for his theory of relativity. Einstein told the story of a dream he had when he was eleven years old. He dreamt "that he was sledding with his friends on a hill near his home. At one point, he was on a sled alone and as he went down the hill, he began going faster and faster. And then he looked up in the sky and saw the sun sending off powerful rays of light as his sled picked up greater and greater speed as if he was approaching the speed of light."

In the interview, the aged Einstein said to Newman, "I think my entire scientific career has been related to my reflection on that dream!"

Overview of some dream interpretation models

The use of dreams is not new. The use of symbolism is not new. Essentially, since the dawn of humankind and across every culture of the world people have looked to the symbolic language of their dreams for guidance. Yet, during the middle and later parts of the twentieth century the practice of using dream guidance fell out of favor, particularly in the Western world -- except in psychoanalytic circles. Now, in modern times interest in dream interpretation is increasing. The following is a brief review of some modern dream interpretation models.

Freudian

This approach bases its techniques of dream interpretation on the observation that the images and feelings we experience in our dreams come from real life experiences and go through a process of condensation, displacement, representation, symbolism, and, finally, secondary revision. Underlying these mechanisms is Freud's contention that dreams are feelings, memories and conflicting emotions appearing to us in disguised forms.

Condensation is the concept that the dream is a compressed version of all the dream-thoughts that arose about a particular theme. Displacement refers to differences in the obvious or manifest dream content from the deeper, hidden and often forbidden dream-thoughts. Representation is the concept that dreams are predominantly visual and sensorial. Symbolism refers to images found more in folklore and myths than in dreams, although consideration of dream symbolism is necessary, as well as some consideration of dreamer's associations. Secondary revision refers to the mind's "secondary" efforts to temper dream contents when a dream escapes the censoring mind and arouses distressing feelings (Freud, 1955, *The Interpretation of Dreams* [J. Strachey, Trans. and Ed.], Basic Book, Inc., Publishers).

Jungian

Jung said, "I have no theory about dream . . . and I am not sure that my way of handling dreams deserves the name of a 'method.' . . . On the other hand, I know that if we meditate on a dream sufficiently long and thoroughly something almost always comes of it" (Jung, 1954, *The Practice of Psychotherapy* [R. F. C. Hull, Trans.], Bollingen Series/Pantheon Books).

Mattoon, Jungian analyst, does present Jung's "method" in steps. Jungian dream interpretation steps as presented by Mattoon are: (1) state the dream text in terms of a structure (setting, plot, and lysis [solution or result]); (2) establish the context of the dream; (3) bring appropriate attitudes to the dream interpretation (nothing can be assumed about the meanings or the images, consider the differences in personality of the dreamer and the interpreter, and realize that the dream is not a disguise but a set of psychic facts); (4) interpret the dream images as either objective or subjective; (5) explore dream for compensatory functions; (6) consider the influence of the dreamer's conscious situation on the dream; (7) and, verify the interpretation by confirmation with the dreamer and by comparison to subsequent dreams and subsequent events (Mattoon, 1984, *Understanding Dreams,* Spring Publishing Company).

Existentialists

Reject or minimize the role of the unconscious and treat dreams as an extension of waking life. Boss, best known of the existentialists for focusing on dreams, looked on dreams in their phenomenal state (Boss, 1958, *The Analysis Of Dreams,* Philosophical Library, Inc., New York).

Culturalism

This takes a social base for interpreting dreams. Bonime emphasizes feelings as probably the most significant expression of any individual's personality (Bonime, 1962, *The Clinical Use Of Dreams,* Basic Books).

Ullman uses the group as the social setting. His group method is composed of four stages: (1) elicit the dream and clarify the dream; (2) the group makes the dream its own; (3) the dreamer's response and working toward closure; and (4) the dreamer's review of the dream (Ullman, "Dreams, The Dreamer, and Society," In G. Delaney [Ed.], 1993, *New Directions in Dream Interpretation,* State University of New York Press).

Gestalt

This derives its format from Perls' original technique of assuming that every element of the dream represents a part of the dreamer's personality. The different parts of the dream represent fragmented parts of the dreamer's personality. To become a unified person, these fragmented parts of the personality that appear in dreams must be re-owned (Perls, 1969, *Gestalt Therapy Verbatim,* Real People Press).

Savary, Berne, and Williams

Their dream interpretation is a four-dimensional approach: psychological, spiritual, historical, and theological. The approach includes thirty primary techniques, most of which seem to be stand-alone techniques. For example, their technique "Title, Theme, Affect, Question" (TTAQ) is used as a method by itself.

The four TTAQ steps are: (1) title the dream; (2) determine the major theme of the dream; (3) identify the dominant affect (emotion) experienced during the dream; and (4) determine what question the dream is trying to help the dreamer become conscious of (Savary, Berne, & Williams, 1984, *Dreams and Spiritual Growth: A Christian Approach To Dreamwork,* Paulist Press).

The Dream Interview (Delaney)

The interviewer, either a dreamwork specialist, or the dreamer herself or himself, conducts an interview to elicit dream meanings. A crucial part of the dream interview method is that the interviewer pretends to come from another planet. In that way, the dreamer is compelled to give his or her own specific associations to the dream. The goal is for the dreamer to interpret the dream from the dreamer's own knowledge, opinions and beliefs, with as few interpretations or explanations from the interviewer as possible (Delaney, 1996, *Living Your Dreams,* HarperCollins).

Bibliography

Allen, David M. *A Family Systems Approach to Individual Psychotherapy*. Northvale, New Jersey: Jason Aronson, Inc., 1994.

Barrett, Deirdre. *The Committee of Sleep*. New York: Crown Publishers, 2001.

Benish, Steven. "Assessing Family Interventions." From *Family Counseling for All Counselors*. Greensboro, North Carolina: Co-publishers -- Eric Clearing house on Counseling and Student Services, American Counseling Association Foundation, 2003, pp. 161-174.

Bible. King James Version. The World Publishing Company, Cleveland and New York.

Bible. Authorized King James Version. Chicago, ILL: Consolidated Book Publishers, 1955.

Bible. Possibility Thinkers New King James Version, edited by Robert H. Schuller. New York: Thomas Nelson Publishers, 1984.

Bible. Good News Bible, with Deuterocanonicals/Apocrypha, Today's English Version. New York: American Bible Society, 1993.

Boushahla, Jo Jean and Reidel-Geubtner, Virginia. *The Dream Dictionary*. New York: Berkley, 1992.

Bulkeley, Kelly.
--*Spiritual Dreaming, A Cross-Cultural and Historical Journey*. Mahwah, New Jersey: Paulist Press, 1995.
-- *An Introduction to the Psychology of Dreaming*. Westport, Connecticut: Praeger, 1997.

Butterworth, Eric. "The School of Life," *Centerpeace*. Vol. 11 - No. 1. New York: The Unity Center of New York, September/October 1996.

Bynum, Edward Bruce.
--*The Family Unconscious*. Wheaton, Illinois: The Theosophical Publishing House, 1984.
--*Families and the Interpretation of Dreams: Awakening the Intimate Web*. Paraview Books, 2003.

Caligor, L., and May, Rollo. *Dreams and Symbols: Man's Unconscious Language*. New York: Basic Books, 1968.

Cartwright Rosalind and Lamberg, Lynne. *Crisis Dreaming, Using Your Dreams to Solve Your Problems*. ASJA Press, an imprint of iUniverse.com, Inc., 2000.

Cirlot, J. E. *A Dictionary of Symbols*. New York: Barnes & Noble Books, 1971.

Delaney, Gayle.
--"The Dream Interview." From *New Directions in Dream Interpretation*, edited by Gayle Delaney. State University of New York Press, 1993, pp. 195-240.
--*Living Your Dreams, The Classic Bestseller on Becoming Your Own Dream Expert*. HarperCollins, 1996.

Duesbury, Evelyn M.
-- "Professor Uses Dreams as Guides in Working with Students." *Dream Network, 13*(2), 24-25, 33.
--"Utilizing Dreams to Understand and Mollify Relationship Issues." University of Wisconsin-Whitewater (Thesis), 2000.
--"Personalized Method for Interpreting Dreams (PMID) -- As applied to relationship issues." *Dreaming: Journal of the Association for the Study of Dreams*, 11(4), 207-216, 2001.
--*The Counselor's Guide for Facilitating the Interpretation of Dreams: Family and Other Relationship Systems Perspectives*. New York: Routledge. November 2010.
--*A Dream-Guided Meditation Model and the Personalized Method For Interpreting Dreams*. New York: Routledge. 2017.
--*Writers' Guiding Dreams*. Spain: Editorial Calliope. 2018.

Duesbury, Evelyn M. and Bynum, Edward Bruce. "Awakening Personal Meanings with Symbol Phrases, Systems Effects, and More." *Dream Network Journal 23*(1), 34-37, 2004.

Faraday, Ann. *The Dream Game*. New York: Berkeley Books, 1974.

Freud, Sigmund. *The Interpretation of Dreams,* translated and edited by J. Strachey. New York: Basic Book, Inc., Publishers, 1955.

Hall, Calvin S. *The Meaning of Dreams*. Harper & Row, 1966.

Hall, James A. *Clinical Uses of Dreams: Jungian Interpretations and Enactments*. New York: Grune & Stratton, Inc., 1977.

Hartmann, Ernest.

--"Making Connections in a Safe Place: Is Dreaming Psychotherapy?" *Dreaming, Journal of the Association for the Study of Dreams* 5(4), 213-228, 1995.

--*Dreams and Nightmares, The Origin and Meaning of Dreams.* Cambridge, Massachusetts: Perseus, 1998.

Hersh, J. B. and Bynum, Edward Bruce. "The Use of Dreams in Brief Therapy." *Psychotherapy: Theory, Research and Practice 22*(5), 1985.

Hill, Clara. E. *Working with Dreams in Psychotherapy.* New York: The Guilford Press, 1996.

Hill, Clara E., Zack, J. S., Wonnell, T. L., Hoffman, M.A., Rochlen, A. B., Goldberg, J. L., Nakayama, E. Y., Heaton, K. J., Kelley, F.A., Eiche, K., Tomlinson, M.J., and Hess, D. "A Structured Brief Therapy with a Focus on Dreams of Loss for Clients with Troubling Dreams and Recent Loss." *Journal of Counseling Psychology, 47,* 90-101, 2000.

Jung, Carl J. *Two Essays on Analytical Psychology,* translated by R. F. C. Hull. Princeton, New Jersey: Bollingen Series/Princeton University Press, 1966.

Jung, Carl J. *The Practice of Psychotherapy.* R. F. C. Hull, Trans., Bollingen Series/Pantheon Books, 1954,

Kelsey, Morton.
--*God, Dreams and Revelation: A Christian Interpretation of Dreams.* Minneapolis: Augsburg, 1991.
--*Transcend, a Guide to the Spiritual Quest.* New York: Crossroad, 1981.

Kramer, Milton. "The Selective Mood Regulatory Function of Dreaming: An Update and Revision." From *The Functions of Dreaming,* edited by A. Moffitt, M. Kramer and R. Hoffman, New York: State University of New York Press, pp. 139-195, 1981.

Kramer, M., Roth, T., Arand, D., and Bonnet, M. "Waking and Dreaming Mentation: A Test of Their Interrelationship." *Neuroscience Letters 22,* 83-86, 1981.

Krippner, Stanley and Dillard, Joseph. *Dreamworking, How To Use Your Dreams for Creative Problem-Solving.* Buffalo, New York: Bearly, 1988.

Krippner, Stanley and Bogzaran, Fariba and Percia de Carvalho, Andre. *Extraordinary Dreams and How to Work with Them.* Albany, New York: State University of New York Press, 2002.

Krippner, Stanley and Jaeger, Christopher and Faith, Laura. "Identifying and Utilizing Spiritual Content in Dream Reports." *Dreaming 11*(3), 127-147, 2001.

Mattoon, Mary Ann. *Understanding Dreams*. Spring Publishing Company, 1984.

May, Rollo. *The Discovery of Being*. New York: W. W. Norton & Company, 1983.

Perls, Fritz. *Gestalt Therapy Verbatim*. Lafayette, California: Real People Press, 1969.

Polster, E., and Polster, M. *Gestalt Therapy Integrated*. New York: Brunner/Mazel Publishers, 1973.

Siegel, Alan B. *Dream Wisdom, Uncovering Life's Answers in your Dreams*. Celestial Arts, 2002.

Spiegel, Sharon Baron, and Hill, Clara. A. "Guidelines for Research on Therapist Interpretation: Toward Greater Methodological Rigor and Relevance to Practice." *Journal of Counseling Psychology 36*(1), 121-129, 1989.

Synesius of Cyrene.

https://www.livius.org/sources/content/synesius/synesius-dreams/

Ullman, Montague and Zimmerman, Nan. *Working With Dreams*. Los Angeles: Jeremy Tarcher, 1979.

Van de Castle, Robert L. *Our Dreaming Mind*. New York: Ballantine Books, 1994.

Wollmering, B. "Dreams and Spirituality, An Historical Perspective." *Dream Time*, a *Publication of the Association for the Study of Dreams,* Spring 1997.

Wolman, Benjamin B. and Ullman, Montague, editors. *Handbook of States of Consciousness*. New York: Van Nostrand Reinhold Company, 1996.

Made in the USA
Las Vegas, NV
04 August 2023

75638743R10125